Keep Pressin'

PRETTY

Kisha Prince

Keep Pressin'
PRETTY

A GUIDE ON HOW TO SLAY FROM THE INSIDE OUT

BY KISHA PRINCE

TUCKER
PUBLISHING HOUSE LLC

Paperback ISBN: 978-1-7377140-5-7
Library of Congress Number: 2021920031

Published 2021 by
Tucker Publishing House, LLC
26056 Van Dyke Ave #3502
Centerline, MI 48015
www.tuckerpublishinghouse.com

Published in the United States of America

DEDICATION

I would like to dedicate Keep Pressin' Pretty: A Guide on How to Slay From the Inside Out to my daughter Naja. You are a fearless boss and a beautiful soul. You are my motivation and inspiration for being a better person every day. I have learned so much while raising you, and your resilience, determination, and ability to not let anything hold you back from fulfilling your dreams makes me so proud. I've always tried to make sure you knew who you were and how valuable you are to me. I have no doubt that you will continue to do great things to impact the world. ~Love Mom

TABLE OF CONTENTS

Pressin' *is slang for Pressing.*

   a.   *the act of exerting a strong pressure*

      b.   *to persevere with or persist* in

Slay (urban dictionary)

  a. *Killed it. Succeeded in something amazing*

PREFACE

To my dearly beloved sister,

I don't know where you are mentally as you transition through your journey, but if you are reading this right now, I implore you to *Keep Pressin' Pretty*! I created the term "Keep Pressin' Pretty" to encourage myself when I felt like giving up and going back into the hole I dragged myself out of after spiraling into a deep depression.

The scriptures that I used to inspire myself that Keep Pressin' Pretty represents is:

- *"I press toward the mark for the prize of the high calling of God in Christ Jesus."* —*Philippians 3:14*

- *"To appoint unto them that mourn in Zion, to give unto them beauty for ashes, the oil of joy for mourning, the garment of praise for the spirit of heaviness; that they might be called trees of righteousness, the planting of the Lord, that he might be glorified."*
  —Isaiah 61:3

I want you to also use these scriptures when you feel like throwing in the towel because you are going to be able to help somebody through their test with your testimony. I know you have been knocked down, and it feels like you've been dragged through the mud while transitioning in your journey. But I'm here to tell you that you are closer to your recovery than you are going back into a recession. God is trying to establish you and make sure your feet are planted firmly for the next chapter of your life. It is not by accident that you came across this book at this point in time. The season you are in may seem like a lonely place, but I promise you are not alone. God allowed me to go through some very rough transitions in my journey as well. I didn't understand them at the time, but after the dust settled and I had time to reflect, I realized it was all for YOU....Yes, YOU! It was for me to walk hand in hand with you in this season of your life and encourage you to be fearless and open to the possibility that you're greater than you think.

As you continue to read this book, I am going to talk you through some of my difficult transitions. I'm going to take you into what I like to call my 'spiritual surgery.' You will see how God opened me up and operated on my heart, mind, and spirit. You will see how I, through God's guidance, worked on myself from the inside out. Of course, with any surgery, there is a lot to expose, but I am willing to do that if it means you getting what you need for your breakthrough and recovery. I am overjoyed and elated to know that my rough, tumultuous, yet enlightening journey thus far was not in vain because it was purposed to help you (succeed) slay in yours.

Keep Pressin' Pretty: A Guide on How to Slay from the Inside Out is not meant to be the be-all and end-all to any situation, but it is just another tool you can add to your armor as you go through your personal journey of peaks and valleys. **It is not a self-help book**, but it is more like a "help yourself" to whatever God presents to you while reading about the lessons and gems he gave to me while walking with Him through my transition.

God saw fit to use me as His vessel and wanted me to use my testimony to give you hope, power, strength, and lessons I learned about God and myself. At the end of the day, I'm just a church girl born and raised, in the sanctuary is where I spent most of my days. (*You like how I remixed Fresh Prince of Bel-Air theme song into a gospel tune... Church people are good for that.*) But for real, I'm no different from you. I don't know your story, but I came from humble beginnings and was blessed that God just so happened to be the foundation on which I was built upon. And if you are anything like me, you like a little ratchet music sometimes, and reality shows, but when stuff hits the fan and your back is against the wall, you know where your help comes from.

So, at this time, I pray that God strengthens, directs, and guides you as you read this book. I pray that you remember that your Heavenly Father loves you very much. And although the adversities of your transition are overwhelming at times, His love is redeeming, protecting, giving, and sanctifying you daily. All the things you will read I didn't get overnight, but it was understood over time.

I hope that you are encouraged and empowered to press beyond your trauma and know that your best days are ahead of you.

Keep Pressin' Pretty
KP

CHAPTER 1

BROKEN ON THE BATTLEFIELD

My prayer for you: *I pray that the suffering of this time is not worthy to be compared to your reward.*

LORD, WHERE ARE YOU?! I had to open up my mental health toolbox and take out every encouraging and motivating quote I ever told myself down through the years. I had to really hang on to every word of every scripture and affirmation for what I was about to embark upon. It's easy to throw out the scriptures and give out inspirational quotes when others come to you with their crisis, but it's a whole other ball game when your faith is being tested, and you're next in line for the fiery furnace.

This was my story when I was transitioning from what I thought would be a lifetime but ended up being a season. I was suddenly placed on a battlefield gearing up for the fight of my life. I was walking into unchartered territory with no light in sight. Darkness was hovering, and I couldn't see my destiny for all the destruction and chaos in front of me. I had no point of reference on the different emotions that would come over me. Not to mention how to deal with those emotions as they came. I knew what the situation was, but didn't quite understand how to respond or which direction I should go. Things were changing quickly, and the turning point would become evident. I just didn't know where it would lead me.

I had gone through several transitions in my many years of living (i.e., marriage, graduating from college, transitioning from one job to another, transitioning into motherhood), but the year 2020 trumped all of those years combined. I had never experienced a transition quite like this. Everything in me was challenged, confused, and left to wonder, what's next? The enormous pressure of the battle was compounded by being confined to my home, having to wear a mask to get groceries, and thinking we were all approaching doomsday with this new pandemic called COVID-19 on the rise.

CNN and Fox News were reporting thousands of deaths around the country from a virus that shocked the world. In the meantime, the enemy had every weapon pointed at my head and my heart. He was out for blood and was ready to show no mercy. He was subtle and cunning in how he contended. I wouldn't surely die in the natural sense, but my mental and spiritual health would take a nosedive. I was in a battle that was trying to take me down from the inside out. The enemy was battling my inner thoughts and tried to use my mind to war against me mentally. I didn't know 2020 would be my year to suffer, but God knew. It didn't take Him by surprise. I was just the person He chose and trusted to get in the fire. The enemy was put on assignment for me well before the pandemic of 2020. Ironically, 2020 was the year that everything would rise to the surface, erupt like a volcano, and then be revealed. I had been in the fire before, but the heat was never this high, and the stakes were even higher.

I sensed the shift taking place in my life, but I was leaning on hope and a prayer. A few years prior, devastation hit my household so hard that it left huge cracks in the infrastructure. I thought we had enough in us to recover and build again, but the construction of our foundation was not strong enough to last. Fast forward, we found ourselves at a crossroad. There were options presented, and decisions made that would change the trajectory of our lives.

Consequently, I lost a 17-year investment that I poured my love, blood, sweat, and tears into. I went through a painful divorce that devastated my family. I lost a part of my legacy that I helped build from scratch. I lost a union that was once the highlight of my life. The turmoil that my family and I suffered left me lost and shattered. I was standing in the midst of the battlefield, looking for solace. It felt like the wind was knocked out of me, and I was holding on for dear life. I was mentally and emotionally declining, and the enemy appeared to be winning the battle. The pain of what happened, and the sense of betrayal ran so deep that I was questioning my own existence. I was questioning why I was still on this earth. I asked God, "What do you want from me?" I felt like I had nothing else to give. I was gearing up to throw in the white flag because the weapons that were formed against me appeared to be prospering. I had so many questions I wanted God to answer, including if He loved me. My faith was teetering, and my spirit needed oxygen. The losses from this battle were more devastating and gut-wrenching than one could ever imagine. I didn't know how I would get past the anguish of this chapter because I lost a part of myself.

Half of me died, and the other half of me didn't know where to begin in trying to open the door to the next chapter of my life. I was in terrible mourning.

I was extremely sad, frustrated, anxious, angry, confused, and severely depressed. Mentally I was in quicksand, and because my mind was in such a sunken place, my body followed suit. My body was not processing the anxiety and depression very well. I would have bad body aches and migraines because I cried and grieved more in the year 2020 than I have in my entire life. I felt like I was spinning out of control. My blood pressure got as high as 175/136. I felt like I was going to implode because I was dealing with every emotion known to man. I went from being on an emotional roller coaster to being in an emotional coma.

In my mind, I couldn't move. The enemy had me just where he wanted me, blinded by the situation, angry at the world, blaming everyone around me, and hanging on to my sanity by a thread. I felt worthless, powerless, and ashamed to think I had a fighting chance of winning this battle. The enemy would be lurking in my mind and patrolling my thoughts. He would tell me not to get out of bed because 'you're too sad.' He would try to convince me that I was a horrible person, and I wasn't good enough to love. 'Your feelings don't matter because nobody cares' is what he would tell me over and over again.

My mental suffering regularly showed up like groundhogs' day. I remember not being able to sleep because my brain wouldn't turn off long enough for me to get any rest. I was fearful about the uncertainties of my future, yet the thought of where I was in the present time was debilitating. My spirit man was flat-lining, and I needed God to give my faith CPR. I needed to press past those negative and self-destructive thoughts that were holding my feet back from moving. God seemed so far off in the distance. I had to somehow connect to God in order to press forward and not die in sorrow. How would I go about doing that? How would I rely on a God whom I thought left me to die on the battlefield? **#keeppressinpretty**

CHAPTER 2

CHECK YOUR CONNECTION

My prayer for you: *I pray that you seek God first and believe that He can do anything but fail.*

HERE I AM! God said I am with you always, even unto the end of the world. I was looking for God in the daylight with a flashlight. That's how much I needed Him. While on the battlefield during my transition, I had to create a sanctuary to refuel and retreat. This is where I went to lay down my burdens and talk to my Savior. This battle taught me many lessons, but one of the greatest lessons was about prayer. I learned how to pray, when to pray, and what it takes to get a prayer through.

At the beginning of my prayer journey, I called it my "meetings of lamentation" with God. They were some of my first counseling sessions before I started seeing my therapist. Initially, I would go into prayer so weak and drained that I could barely stay on my knees without going prostrate. I would just lay before the Lord in groaning and full of tears. In those moments, I just wanted to be in the presence of someone I knew who loved me unconditionally. I just wanted to escape from the world and hide behind my Heavenly Father. I would sit before Him speechless and confused, trying to wrap my mind around the devastation and my life-changing so drastically.

Initially, I didn't have the spiritual or mental capacity to give any long eloquent apostolic prayer. I finally understood what the mothers of the church meant when they said, "When I couldn't say a word, I just raised my hands."

In my ongoing "meetings of lamentation" with God, I would constantly remind Him that I needed His help to get through the pain. Pain and shame were dragging me down a never-ending dark hole. I would ask Him to guide my footsteps, because the thought of what was on the other side of this chapter was daunting and ambiguous in my mind. You would think transitioning into a new chapter would be exciting, but my pain and acrimony had me blinded to the possibilities. I just wanted God to come down from heaven, swoop me up out of the fiery furnace, strike down my enemies, take away the pain, open up the windows of heaven and pour down a blessing I didn't have room enough to receive. Yes, Saints, I wanted God to give me the religious special supersized with extra blessings on the side. However, what I wanted and what I needed looked like two different things. God knew that what He was going to do for me would not only help me for this season but sustain me in the seasons to come.

I remember tossing and turning in the middle of many nights, wrestling with my thoughts and pacing the floor. It seemed like all my agony worsened in the midnight hour. I would ask God, "Am I losing my mind?" I felt like I was going crazy. Pacing the floor ended in me being in a fetal position, rocking in the corner of my room. I was looking for joy in the morning because weeping endured all night. I desperately needed refuge and deliverance after leaving all I had on the battlefield. I was trying to pray the angels down from heaven. I was praying in His name, rebuking the enemy, making my request known, and speaking in other tongues as the Spirit gave utterance. I was praying in the morning and sometimes all night long, so I just knew I was reaching the throne and shaking things up in the heavens. I constantly prayed because prayer changes things, right?

I was communicating and seeking God's face, so why did I still feel defeated? Why was I still severely depressed and fearful? Why was I easily frustrated and filled with anxiety, wondering how I was going to make it? Here I was doing my good praying, but nothing was changing in my life. I felt like I was a hamster on a wheel making no progress. Was God listening to me? Did He care to answer my prayers? Have you ever felt like you were going in circles in prayer? Keep it real. Have you ever felt like prayer just wasn't working? This was another ploy the enemy used while I was on the battlefield. These were the mind games he played when he knew I was mentally and emotionally susceptible to his deception. Whenever we have those types of questions and thoughts in our minds, the first thing the enemy likes to do is persuade us to fault God for not answering our prayers. I can admit that I passive-aggressively blamed God, but all along, there was something to be said about me and the way I went about seeking Him.

All my life, I just heard "pray about it!!" So, it was a hard pill for me to swallow when I discovered that my prayers were hitting the ceiling and they weren't anywhere near heaven, let alone reaching the Holy of Holy's (bless my heart). I was checking off all the boxes in prayer, or so I thought. True enough, I was kneeling, but the question is, "Was I plugged in and connecting to God?" I had to take a step back and measure how I was praying to what God's word says about seeking Him. The bible says, "And all things, whatsoever ye shall ask in prayer, believing, ye shall receive." (Matt 21:22)

Though I am a multifaceted woman with many different layers and dimensions to myself, at the end of the day, I'm a church girl at heart, so I knew that prayer worked, and I know the bible says we should always pray. However, the overarching component that was missing and making me wonder why I wasn't making any headway in prayer was my FAITH. I was missing the main ingredient that made God rise to the occasion. Interestingly enough, I had faith to get on my knees and pray, and after, I felt relieved in that moment, but I didn't have faith when I got off my knees going about my daily life. Before the day was over, I was weak, discouraged, and dragging back to my prayer closet, looking for another fix.

I was unconsciously going through the motions of prayer, but not truly believing God for what I was praying for, or believing I was worthy enough for

Him to do it for me. When I look back on it, I shake my head. It's amazing how you can read God's word, go to church all your life, but find out the word wasn't hidden in your heart to apply it to everyday life. Remember when I told you I laid my burdens down in the sanctuary? Well, apparently, I picked them bad boys back up and carried them around. It was evident in how I was behaving outside of my prayer closet that my faith was at an all-time low. My lack of faith cut off the frequency I had with God. I thought God was giving me the silent treatment because He had bigger fish to fry than to hear my cry. But that was absolutely not the case.

Hebrew 11:6, NIV says, and without faith, it is impossible to please God because anyone who comes to him must believe that he exists and that he rewards those who earnestly seek him.

Our mind can be so focused on what we're going through, and how the situation is making us feel that we think God is distant from us, but in actuality, our distractions and unbelief make us distant from Him. Our faith gets smaller and smaller because our situation gets greater and greater in our minds. We give all of our attention to our problem and stop paying attention to the Problem Solver. I was praying these long agonizing prayers to God and then turned around and went back to focusing on the situation and being fearful. Faith and fear cannot coexist in God. It's like oil and water; it just doesn't mix. Just because I prayed without ceasing doesn't mean I was connected to God in the spiritual realm to affect the natural place I was in. God was always being true to His word and could only be elicited by faith. I was the one praying religiously but lacked the faith to manifest and shift my atmosphere. You can say I had a slight power outage. If you try cutting on your television and it won't cut on, you don't just sit there and look at a blank screen. The first thing you do is check to see if it's plugged in, and that's what I had to do.

Are you plugged in, or do you need to check your connection? Have you checked your faith frequency levels lately? Are you operating on a low vibration and need a boost? I challenge you to believe God for what you need and want while you are transitioning on your journey. I dare you to dig deeper and plug in to make that spiritual connection. I dare you to have faith in God even when it doesn't look like things are ever going to change. I dare you to believe God when you are alone, and there is no one there to tell you "it's going to be okay." I dare you to believe God when the choir isn't singing, the preacher isn't preaching, and the church doors are closed. If this pandemic didn't teach us anything, it taught us that nothing is promised, but God. If we are not able to congregate in a sanctuary and have a Wednesday night bible class, then what are you going to do? Will you be connected even when the religious protocols are not in place? God is looking for us to be plugged in and ready to take off our Sunday's best and put on our clothes for combat. Your faith is your first line of defense. So, stay plugged in, so you don't have to get plugged in. *#keeppressinpretty*

CHAPTER 3

I HUNG UP MY DRESS AND HEELS FOR BOOTS AND FATIGUES

My prayer for you: *I pray that you put on the whole armor of God during this trial on the battlefield.*

I TRUST YOU, LORD. After so long of going before God and seeking His face, I remember there being a shift in my prayer meetings. In the beginning, I looked at my prayer meetings as "meetings of lamentation" with God, because I always went to Him in terrible sorrow and weeping. After such a terrible storm in my life, my house had no power due to a lack of faith. I was praying, but I was still operating in the dark. But do I have any witnesses that know that the power doesn't have to stay out forever? God and I restored the power line between the two of us, and the power outage was eventually restored by the surge of my faith. Faith is the generator. It is what causes the current to spark the connection between you and God. It triggers Him and ignites you to do great things. Instead of calling the electric company, God wanted me to start calling those things as though they were. He wanted me to command my soul to bless Him. He wanted me to command my mind to believe Him. He wanted me to command my hands to praise Him. He wanted me to use the power of my tongue to call things into existence.

When I started truly believing God and plugging in through faith, I no longer felt depressed and anxious. I no longer went into "meetings of lamentation" with God, but I went into "meetings of praise and thanksgiving." There was a revival in my spirit that changed my way of thinking. When faith is infused in your prayer, there is a confidence you have that should make your walk change, your attitude change, and your language change. You start believing in what you can do through God because He said, "Behold, I give unto you power to tread on serpents and scorpions, and over all the power of the enemy: and nothing shall by any means hurt you." (Luke 10:19)

It was on and poppin'. I hung up my dress and heels and put on my boots and fatigues. I had to get dressed for the occasion. I had to take back my authority and no longer play these fearful games with the enemy. It was time-out for being cute and civil. II Corinthians 10:4 says, "For the weapons of our warfare are not carnal, but mighty through God to the pulling down of strongholds." My weapon of mass destruction was faith in God's word and my obedience to it. I put the enemy on notice. He could no longer live rent-free in my mind. He could not continue to use my mind as his playground. The word says, "And be not conformed to this world: but be ye transformed by the renewing of your mind, that ye may prove what is that good, and acceptable, and perfect, will of God." (Romans 12:2)

I no longer approached the battlefield from a place of defeat, but I confronted it with praise. I did like Joshua and the Israelites when God told Joshua to take the city of Jericho by walking around it six times, shouting and giving honor unto God. The enemy wasn't expecting this approach to combat. I started thanking God for what He was doing, what He had done, and what He was going to do in my future. The bible says, "Let us, therefore, come boldly to the throne of grace, that we may obtain mercy and find grace to help in time of need." (Hebrews 4:16). I went from being docile and distressed in prayer to bold and believing. I stopped asking God to give me a plan, and I started giving God my plans and goals for Him to anoint and expand. I actually went into prayer with something for God to bless instead of going empty-handed. And guess what? I was no longer getting an echo when I prayed due to lack of faith, but my connection was strong enough for me to get insight and foresight into the wonderful things God had in stored for my life. I was able to tap into God in a way that I had never experienced before. I went to God with high expectations. When I prayed, it wasn't a matter of if God could do it, but it was a matter of when. Why would I go to such a big God with such a small request? Matthew 16:19 says, "I will give you the keys of the kingdom of heaven; whatever you bind on earth will be bound in heaven, and whatever you loose on earth will be loosed in heaven."

I told God I needed to obtain the keys to the kingdom of heaven. I had some things I needed to do and strongholds I needed to tear down, so that was going to require the keys.

I remember trying to sell our family home in the middle of the pandemic. We put the house on the market and had to leave home every time a potential buyer came to view it because of the virus. There were over 50 people who came to view the home in a matter of two months. I had been praying and praying for the house to sell, but there were no offers. I was praying but doubtful at the same time, because I knew the house needed some major repairs. In the back of my mind, I didn't see someone buying it with so many flaws. What I love about God is He is merciful and patient with us even in our ignorance. God was always so compassionate and kind to me, especially at those low faith moments. In His infinite wisdom, He had already made provisions for those moments I fell short.

After God dealt with me about my faith and I really started moving and thinking differently, He used my intuition to reveal things to me that were going on in the spirit realm about my house. I remember having a keen sense of contrary, negative spirits in the atmosphcrc of the home. It wasn't what I would call a normal atmosphere for my home. God moved upon me to start making as many minor improvements to the house as I could. He told me as clear as day to begin saying in the atmosphere, "This house is going to sell." I started decreeing,

"The house is going to sell" multiple times a day throughout the house. I remember playing Yolanda Adams, "*The battle is not yours*," and "*In the midst of it all*," amongst other anointed songs to create an atmosphere of worship in my house.

After so long, God moved some things in the spiritual realm while I was doing what He told me in the natural realm, and in two weeks, there was an offer on the house. Two months after that, it sold. It makes me cry just thinking about it, because God proved Himself to be true when I trusted him. I was loosening things on earth as they were being loosed in heaven. I was able to shift the atmosphere back to one that was conducive to the presence of God by commanding my tongue to speak the words God told me to speak.

Jude 20-25—
20 But ye, beloved, building up yourselves on your most holy faith, praying in the Holy Ghost,
21 Keep yourselves in the love of God, looking for the mercy of our Lord Jesus Christ unto eternal life.

22 And of some have compassion, making a difference:

23 And others save with fear, pulling them out of the fire; hating even the garment spotted by the flesh.

24 Now unto him that is able to keep you from falling, and to present you faultless before the presence of his glory with exceeding joy,

25 To the only wise God our Savior, be glory and majesty, dominion and power, both now and ever. Amen.

On the battlefield, I learned that when you pray, you are going into partnership with God. You are not going to Him just so He can dry all your tears and take all your request. You are not going to Him, so He can give you everything you ask for, and you offer Him nothing in return. You are going to Him, letting Him know that you are willing to put your hands in His hands and agree on what His word says about Him and about yourself. You are going to God with praise and with an attitude of worship, soliciting His wisdom and guidance on how to maneuver on the battlefield. You want God to know that you are willing and able to put in the work under His supervision. God said faith without works is dead. (James 2:14-26) Therefore, I had to not only believe Him, but I had to put my hand to the plow and do what He asked me to do. I had to put my feelings about my situation to the side momentarily for the sake of putting His will before my own to get things done on the battlefield. There is a time and place for everything, and God let me know that it wasn't time to be in my feelings, crying while in battle. It was time for warfare in the spiritual to get things done in the natural.

A great example of putting your feelings aside for the greater good is found in Matthew 26:39-45 when it was close to Jesus having to lay down His life for our sins. It talks about Jesus falling on His face and praying, "O my Father, if it be at all possible, let this cup pass from me: nevertheless, not as I will, but as thou will be done." Jesus being God wrapped in flesh, knew that He had a huge undertaking baring the cross, but He had to ignore His flesh and put His feelings to the side to get the job done. Otherwise, we would all be dead in our sins.

When I took my focus off the issue at hand and put my feelings to the side to deal with later, I saw things begin to change. Not only in how I approached God in prayer but how I approached my situation. I prayed God's word over my life and directly to the devil's face.

I DECLARED....

His word says, Now unto Him, that is able to keep you from falling, and to present you faultless before the presence of His glory with exceeding joy (Jude 1:24). That let me know that I wasn't guilty in His eyes because His blood was strong enough to cover a multitude of my sins through repentance and put them in the sea of forgetfulness. So, I no longer went into prayer from a place of guilt and shame, but I went from a place of power and redemption.

His word says that "Ye are of God, little children, and have overcome them: because greater is He that is in you, than he that is in the world." (I John 4:4) This let me know that I had the victory even when the odds were stacked against me. So, when I went into prayer, I was not going to ask God what He could do; I was going in prayer thanking Him for what He's already done.

His word says I can do all things through Him that strengthens me. (Philippians 4:13). This let me know that anything I set in my mind to do with the willingness to put in the work and God as my leader, I could accomplish all those things.

Listen!!! By reading His Word and applying it to my life, it pretty much let me know that I was in a fixed fight!!! The devil didn't stand a chance. The devil wanted me to throw in the towel and wave the white flag, but after I trusted God and resisted the enemy, he cowered off the battlefield. He didn't have power over my mind or my situation. His weapons would not prosper just like the Word says. God was and is always in control. Remember that. *#keeppressinpretty*

CHAPTER 4

THE ASSIGNMENTS

My prayer for you: *I pray that God heals you and makes you whole.*

After all I'd been through in the process of my transition, I finally made my very sad exodus from a chapter that lasted 17 years to anticipating a new chapter that was full of promise. Things were fresh and not that far removed, so I still had my fatigues and combat boots just in case a sister still had more beef with the enemy. I closed the door to a very sad milestone that literally changed my life. I got out without any wounds that could be seen with the naked eye, but there were some deep psychological wounds that were still raw and easily triggered. I was going through the aftershocks of all the circumstances that took place. I intentionally left some things behind that I couldn't take into my next chapter, but I brought some bags with me that I just wasn't ready to get rid of so quickly. I was still holding on to some things I was trying to make sense of. My heart was irregular from the break it suffered. I was wrapping my mind around being single after operating as one with another person for so long. I felt like a large part of me had died. I had to figure out how I would get back to being a whole person again.

Psychological wounds leave an imprint on your heart and mind. It is wounds that sometimes keep us captive to a certain period in time. Have you ever listened to an old song or remembered a historical event that automatically took you back in time? You remember what you were doing and who you were with when the song was playing or when the event happened. This is an example of having psychological wounds that haven't healed. The difference is you are physically going from year to year, but mentally you are trapped in the time when you were mentally scarred. When we hold on to that hurt and refuse to release it, it's like being psychologically imprisoned by it. It holds you hostage to the pain, and you become accustomed to being locked down by it. We hide behind it, and it becomes what we use as a defense mechanism when God is trying to pull us out. It's the addiction we didn't know we had if we were not careful.

I like to think of it as being stuck on Pain Street. When God is trying to pick us up to take us to Joy Road, we buck up against Him because the pain has us in bondage. Pain and shame are no longer just how we feel, but it becomes the means by which we function in life. You can get so used to the dysfunction of it that it takes control over your present, constantly reminds you of your past, and hinders you from progressing into your future. And although we don't like the way it feels, our enslaved minds find excuses to wallow in it longer.

I thought that in order for the pain to go away, I was supposed to be vindicated. I thought justice was supposed to be served. I wanted the people that caused my pain to be the ones to make it right. I was predicating my healing on something that was outside of my control. Deuteronomy 32:35 (ESV) says, "Vengeance is mine, and recompense, for the time when their foot shall slip; for the day of their calamity is at hand, and their doom comes swiftly." I had to remember that the goal was not to get revenge or make people see things the way I saw them, but the goal was to heal.

Get rid of all bitterness, rage and anger, brawling and slander, along with every form of malice. Be kind and compassionate to one another, forgiving each other, just as in Christ God forgave you. — Ephesians 4:31-32, NIV

For what I was trying to accomplish in this new chapter, bitterness would not have looked good on me, and spite would have messed up my swag. I wanted to see myself from a place of wholeness and not from a place of brokenness. I spoke to a dear friend of mine who went through something similar to what I went through, and she said, "Give yourself the grace and time you need to heal." I held on to that, because healing is an ongoing process. There were so many layers to work through and repair. I knew this would not happen overnight or when people thought it should. I needed quality healing and not a speedy recovery. So, I took my time and really worked at it.

My healing started when I surrendered my pain to the process of healing. I decided to go to counseling. Proverbs 11:14 (ESV) says, "Where there is no guidance, a people fall, but in an abundance of counselors there is safety." Please don't be afraid to seek out professional help. Therapy was one of the things that God used to help stabilize and even helped me with things I suppressed from my childhood. Counseling was my bridge over trouble waters. It was a necessary method used for me to verbalize my thoughts in a safe space while getting sound advice on how to work through the trauma. Counseling helped me sift through the chaos left in my mind after such a tremendous tragedy.

As some of you may know, the trauma of divorce or separation of the family has different stages to it, and the aftershocks can sometimes be worse than the initial disaster. I felt like I needed counsel for every stage. Initially, my sessions were just like my "meetings of lamentation." It seems as though I would just dump on her every problem, story, and complaint I had. I would uncontrollably cry myself through some sessions and be numb in others. I felt like I was handcuffed to what I went through. Although I was physically removed from the situation, my mind and heart were in a holding cell. What's crazy about that was, the keys to release my mind and my heart was in my hands. God had given me the power to release myself, but I wasn't ready to unlock the cell and go free.

Time!!! Time was part of the antidote to my healing. As I continued to go to therapy and sought after my healing, I noticed myself getting calmer and calmer in each session. I saw the transformation of myself steadily transpiring. I saw brokenness turn to wholeness over time. It was such a blessing to see my evolution. God was so patient and gentle with me the whole time during this process that I am forever grateful. He was indeed gracious and merciful, but He didn't let me off the hook. He gave me some tough love and held my feet to the fire. He let me know I had some assignments to do to get the desired results He wanted.

The three most fundamental things that were asked of me that got me closer to my healing were forgiveness, overcoming the pain, and doing self-care.

Forgiveness: "And when you stand praying, if you hold anything against anyone, forgive them, so that your Father in heaven may forgive you your sins." (Mark 11:25)

Overcome the pain: "Trust in the Lord with all your heart, and do not lean on your own understanding." (Proverbs 3:5)

Self-Care: And He said to them, "Come away by yourselves to a desolate place and rest awhile." For many were coming and going, and they had no leisure even to eat." (Mark 6:31)

Forgiveness

The first assignment I had was to **forgive**. I know you've heard the saying, "forgiving is not for the other person, but it's for you." This saying doesn't make it easier to do, but it's true nevertheless. I'm going to keep it all the way real with you. My ego would not allow me to forgive initially. I needed to feel justified. I needed something that brought me some sort of consolation after going through the hell I had been through. So, holding a grudge was the prize I took away from something that left me so hurt. In my mind, I thought that not forgiving was my way of maintaining some sort of control. However, going to counseling helped me to realize that if I didn't forgive, I was giving my transgressor the power over me. They have power over your feelings, emotions, and your will to heal. Forgiveness is the first step of taking your power back. When you forgive, you exchange forgiveness for your power. The more I forgave, the more I healed. Trust me, it did not happen overnight, but over some time, I was able to release the pain, forgive those whom I thought wronged me, and move on. I had to put what was done to me in my past in order for me to progressively move forward.

By forgiving, I disarmed the transgressor of my power and lifted the burden I was carrying off of me. Remember those bags I said I just couldn't get rid of from my last chapter? I was carrying those bags of disappointment and shame around for too long. In addition to forgiving my transgressors, I had to forgive myself. One of those bags I was carrying around was for me. It was a bag filled with the shame and guilt of what I should have done or what I could have done better. It was for the pain I caused from being pained. I had to unpack those things and get rid of the regret, humiliation, guilt, and other emotions that had me bound to my past. I had already asked God to forgive me, but I was still holding on to everything He forgave. I had to remember that He presented me faultless before the presence of His glory with exceeding joy.

'I will restore your health, and I will heal your wounds,' declares the Lord. —Jeremiah 30:17 NIV

Overcome the pain

My second assignment was to **overcome the pain.** This was the time to deal with all the feelings I had to push aside in prayer to get some things accomplished. This was my opportunity to acknowledge my pain, talk it out with my therapist and also find new perspectives on how to relinquish it. I quickly found out that just because you forgive someone or even yourself doesn't mean you won't still feel the effects of what happened. It's just like someone in recovery after a car accident. Just because their leg is stitched up and their surgery went well doesn't mean they're not going to still feel the agony of what they've experienced. You have to settle into your recovery. While walking this journey in recovery, I needed to fully process the devastation and calamity of what happened to my family and me. This mental anguish was like a fully loaded gun that I had to unload before it did some major damage.

Now I empathize with people who find themselves in reckless situations and don't care about the consequences of their actions. They are more than likely acting out or projecting their pain onto society. I had to examine my pain and make a decision to hold on to it or let it go. My healing was only going to be manifested if I started looking at myself through a new pair of glasses. While transitioning, my vision was very near sided, and I had a narrow lens. I could only see myself attached to my pain. Like the saying goes, I couldn't see the forest for the tree right in front of me. God had to broaden my vision so I could see myself as healed and free.

I'm a human being, so it was natural to feel pain, but it was unhealthy for me to succumb to it and let it have power over me. There was so much possibility beyond my pain, but before I could take advantage of those possibilities, I had to be unchained from the pain. God wanted me to not only heal and overcome the pain, but He wanted me to be made whole. He wanted me to stop wrestling with it, move forward and start building. He knew I had work to do, but I had to be whole to do it. He had already given me the power to defeat it, but I had to see myself as delivered.

Even though I was walking this journey with my feet, my willingness to press towards my healing started in my mind. God revised my vision and opened up my spiritual eye. I no longer blamed the people around me for how I felt or for what I thought they did wrong. God gave me a new perspective and showed me the real culprit that was pulling the strings. He used Ephesians 6:12 that says, "For we wrestle not against flesh and blood, but against principalities, against powers, against the rulers of the darkness of this world, against spiritual wickedness in high places." The enemy's tactics were diabolical. He came to kill, steal and destroy everything around me. On the top of his agenda was my faith. He wanted to destroy my ability to trust God. You have to remember that the enemy does not care about your house, your car, your job, or your family. When he comes for you, those things are all collateral damage during the war to destroy your faith. He wants to take the very thing that connects you to God. I was either going to let go of the anger, relieve myself from the hurt, take back my joy, and be at peace, or I was going to be bitter, broken, and die in sorrow. God left that choice up to me.

God knows I wanted to live in peace and have joy. Why should I allow people to take my joy and peace when they weren't the ones to give it to me? When

I made up my mind to press past the heartbreak and pain, God sanctioned me. I was starting to walk in my healing which began to engineer my thoughts and affected my actions. I gave less energy to the negativity of the situation. I was less and less triggered by hearing certain things that would have taken me over the edge previously. I actually started praying that God blesses those who despitefully used me. There was such a peace in that. My mind was becoming more liberated with every decision to release the pain. God has given me the strength and the fortitude to overcome, and I do my best to diligently choose to be an overcomer every day.

Self-Care

The third assignment I had was to **self-care**. This was a new term for me coined during the pandemic of 2020. I hadn't heard the term before then. In the context of what I was going through, self-care was like taking myself through rehab. Divorce or any breakdown of the family structure can leave a person with Post-Traumatic Stress Disorder (PTSD). In the beginning, self-care for me was just taking a breather and calming my spirit. After what seemed like the fight of my life, sitting still in God's presence was just what the doctor ordered. I tried to empty my mind (which is hard to do at first) of everything and relieve all the pressure. It was a calming technique that helped my mind restore itself. Sometimes we can be so restless and high-strung that we need to calm down our inner self. Dealing with this life-changing transition threw my body and mind into a state of shock. It significantly altered the way I thought about myself and how I began to live my life. It affected how I viewed the world. I found myself very guarded and protective of my space. It was important that I gave my mind and body time to recalibrate from the trauma. I had to do things that were surrounded by peace and centered in tranquility. It had to be comforting to my spirit and restorative to my mind. I also had to make time to laugh and get back to my joyous, fun self. I had cried and come down on myself for so long that laughter had become foreign to me. It was easy for me to self-isolate and close myself off to people, but while doing self-care, I was encouraged to go out to dinner with friends periodically and do things socially I hadn't done during my transition. I wanted to be around positive, energetic people that brought peace with them. I didn't need anyone around me using my life as a spectator sport so they could do commentary. It was important for me to have a community of people around me that contributed to my healing and knew how to reach God on my behalf.

When I was alone, I still wanted to feel connected to something. I thought that a divorce social network would help me, and it did. I was able to bond and share stories with women who were in the same boat I was in. It was interesting to hear the different stories from such a diverse group of women, and at the end of the day, we pretty much wanted the same thing, and that was peace of mind. God and I continued with our "meetings of praise and thanksgiving." Whether it was going through my house praising him with Tamela Mann or listening to motivational videos by Miles Monroe (RIP) and Joyce Meyers every day on the way to work and on the way home. God would use my own tongue to speak healing over my wounds. I would speak words of encouragement over myself every day to stay empowered. I repeated to myself every day, "Where I was in my past, can't determine where I am going in my future." "Your latter days will be greater than your former days."

Do me a favor and take some time to speak these words over your life and watch how freeing you begin to feel. Not only speak them but believe every word.

- *I am who God says I am*
- *I can do all things through Christ*
- *I am more than a conquer through Christ Jesus*
- *I will overcome*
- *I am going to live and not die*

- *I am not my mistakes*

- *I am above and not beneath*

Words are powerful. What you hear is a gateway to your thinking, and your thoughts dictate behavior. Proverbs 23:7 says, "For as he thinks in his heart, so is he: Eat and drink, saith he to thee; but his heart is not with thee." I felt my fragile mind getting stronger and stronger. I had to guard my mind and protect my peace at all costs because the enemy was always looking for cracks to slither through to cast doubt and fear. I also started journaling; hence the book you are reading now. I had come to the point where I didn't have any more tears, so I put the emotion behind the pen and had to make this book cry out for me. That was a therapeutic way to release how I felt and use writing as an outlet. You never know how God will use your story for His glory.

God showed me that healing was already in me; I just had to tap into it and stop focusing on the things I had no control over. Just like our bodies heal themselves, our minds can do the same if we

45

surrender our will to God's will. Some of you have been given assignments by God to get you closer to your healing. He is standing by, waiting on you to make the first move. Your pain wants to keep you stuck, but God wants to transition you out into your beautiful destiny. He wants to heal you, but you are going to have to press pass some things, just like the woman with the issue of blood. The bible explains how the woman suffered from a blood condition for twelve years, but one day she pressed through a crowd of people to touch the hem of Jesus's garment for her healing. I can imagine her not only pressing through the crowd but pressing through embarrassment, pressing through the pain, pressing through fear, and pressing pass her past just to connect to Jesus. She was one person in the midst of hundreds, but her faith pushed her to the front of the line and made her whole. Imagine her just showing up in the crowd and not making contact with Jesus. Some of us are just satisfied being associated with Jesus or just being in the crowd of people who know Him and are not willing to do what it takes to connect to Him for ourselves. Like that woman, your faith has to be relentless to get what you desire out of God. I promise that if you stay the course and do the work, you will be healed.

Many times, we are not growing because we are not healing. So many people are suffering emotionally because they haven't dealt with and healed from their past hurt, abuse, rejection, abandonment, etc. Instead of talking about it, they internalize it and bury it in the depths of their soul. And just like the "Walking Dead," those emotions are triggered and resurrected through behavior. If we don't heal, we will transfer the trauma to those we love the most. God desires for us to be whole. He wants us to be balanced and mentally fit. Over the years, we've been putting Band-Aids on things that required stitches and therapy. We need closure on things that have been left wide open. We have confused coping with healing.

If you are suffering from any type of mental disturbances, whether it's depression, stress, anxiety, or any other disorder big or small, I pray that God heals you and delivers you in the name of Jesus! I'm a living witness that you don't have to suffer. God has given us so many ways to find our healing, but we must go after it.

Matthew 7:7 says, "Ask, and it shall be given you; seek, and ye shall find; knock, and it shall be opened unto you."

I decree and declare that after your healing, you will be able to use your past as an outline and not let it define your overall story. You are going to be enlightened to walk in the power you received by doing the assignments God told you to do for your healing. ***#keeppressinpretty***

CHAPTER 5

FIX YO WIG AND PRESS THROUGH THE PROCESS

My prayer for you: I pray that you are a better person coming out of the process than you were going in.

I know you're frustrated, tired, and apprehensive about the process of your transition. Whether it's in your relationship, trying to get your degree, opening up a business, or trying to recover from something very traumatic. Whatever it is you're being transitioned in or out of can cause you to be weary. I didn't know the magnitude and the essence of "Keep Pressin' Pretty" until I thought I had no more press left in me. I was in the process of figuring out my life after divorce while trying to heal from a great blow to my heart. My life was in disarray, and I was trying to navigate through the chaos with some type of order. My brain operates best with structure. I'm that person that has to know where I'm going and how I'm getting there, so when God called Himself mixing things up and giving me an Abram experience, I was like, okay, God, what's going on? I thought I would have a new place to stay immediately after a long, drawn-out process of selling my marital home I had lived in for 13 years, but things didn't go like I thought. I had to put all my belongings in storage and figure out where I was going to live. I'm not going to lie; I was scared. Picture me as a newly single woman with a reduced income, in the beginning stages of a pandemic, looking crazy in a mask and homeless. I knew God was taking me out of my comfort zone, but baybay, I didn't get the homeless memo. God sent me out into the unknown with one suitcase and a dream. He took away everything I was used to and put me in a position that made me have to rely on Him and Him only. I was like, okay God, you know I don't normally roll like this, what do I do from here? I just went through the most devastating time of my life; haven't I suffered enough? God reminded me of Matthew 6:26-34. In a nutshell, He said if I can provide for the birds, take care of the lilies and the grass in the field, how much more valuable are you, my daughter?

At the time, it was a process during my journey I wish I could have time traveled through. I just wanted to go from the problem to the solution and bypass everything in between. I didn't know what was on the other side of the process, and I didn't know if it was worth the end result. But guess what? God said fix yo wig and press through the process. Don't you love when God uses your vernacular and tone to gather you and get you together?

I remember talking on the phone with a friend about what I was going through and how I was feeling, and she told me, "Feelings are not facts." "You can press through this!"

When I told God that I was too weak to press past the way I felt, He said, "I know." Matthew 26:41 says, "Watch and pray that ye enter not into temptation; the spirit is indeed willing, but the flesh is weak." God knew there was no good thing in my flesh, but there was something great in my spirit. He knew there was something great for me in the next chapter of my life if only I could just press pass the weakness of my flesh and the disarray of my emotions. When my friend would always tell me, "You have to press through this," God was speaking to me through her. He wasn't telling my body/flesh to press, but He was instructing my spirit to press. He wanted my spirit to keep pressing towards my purpose through faith. God is the Author and the Finisher of our faith. Once my faith was aligned with my spirit, He knew my flesh would obey. When my legs were weak and my body was limp, He gave my spirit the will to surpass my physical state and give strength to my weakest parts.

He knew deliverance was in my press; progress was in my press; a breakthrough was in my press; new opportunities were in my press.

You can do it!! Don't *try* to do it; just do it! Make it happen! Stop complaining!! Stop saying life is unfair. Stop feeling sorry for yourself! Stop overthinking it!! Just stop it!! That's what I had to tell myself when I was bumming it on my grandmother's couch and spending weeks in a hotel room to get to God's promise.

Yes, I was in unfamiliar territory and going through some of the lowest times of my life, but I got to a fork in the road in my struggle where I either was going to give up, or I was going to trust God. I had come too far to give up now. I was tired of being sick and tired, so wherever God was taking me, I was down for the ride. Plus, I was kind of reaping what I sowed in prayer when I asked God to take me to the next level and expand my territory in my next chapter, so I couldn't be resentful by the way in which He chose to do it.

We can try to abandon the process to get straight to the promise, but if you know anything about walking with God, you know He is not big on overnight successes. Think about all the great people in the bible that God performed mighty works and miracles through. From Abraham, Moses, and Joseph with that sharp coat of many colors to Elijah, Paul, and Jesus himself. None of them achieved greatness or were the people they would eventually become without going through something. So, what made me think God was going to let me slide by without going through the process?

Being confident of this very thing, that he which hath begun a good work in you will perform it until the day of Jesus Christ: —Philippians 1:6

Getting to know God in the process

God doesn't circumvent the journey for the destination. He understands all too well the importance of what that journey entails and what that journey is going to do for you by the time you reach your destination. He takes you through the scenic routes because He wants you to be in the moment and find appreciation and gratitude in the process. He is not necessarily looking at the destination, but He is looking at who you are *becoming* while getting there.

God's focus is you. You are His main priority; that's how much He loves you. It may not feel like it, but the process was designed with your best interest in mind. I didn't understand this until I was out of the fire. Your foresight is 20/20 when you are able to see yourself the way God always saw you. When I was in the midst of the fiery furnace, I didn't see God chipping away at my insecurities and burning off my infirmities. I didn't see Him operating on my mind and giving me a heart transplant. He was peeling back the different layers of who I was to get to what He was calling me to be. Going through the fire was par for the course because we tend to depend on Him more when there are tests and trials to overcome. My strength, courage, and wisdom didn't come at the end of my journey, but it came from the *process* of my journey.

And we know that all things work together for good to them that love God, to them who are the called according to his purpose. —Romans 8:28

The process is where I really got to know God and the power of His might. I didn't get more religious going through the process, but I got in a better relationship with God in the process. God and I were cooler than ever. In my personal walk with God, He was using my process of transition to build this beautiful relationship that required some give and take. It is just like being in any healthy relationship, I was giving and taking, and He was giving and taking in the relationship.

His glory united with my story made a perfect bonding experience. Both of our loves were being proven in the relationship. The love was not shown only in good times but demonstrated at the more challenging times of our relationship. He loved me when I was the worst version of myself and when I wasn't worthy of being loved. He loved me when I didn't choose Him, but I chose my own desires. By the same token, I chose to love Him when He didn't come when I called Him, or I didn't get everything I asked for when I asked for it. I thank God my relationship with him is not 50/50 or competitive in any way because I could never beat God in giving or 'out love' Him. The beauty about God in all His relationships is that He is always the one who gives more because He is the stabilizer and example of true love. God let me know that the purpose of the process is for me to be a better person coming out than I was going in.

God knew that if He had taken me out of the fire before I was ready, I wouldn't be the strong and confident woman I am today. If you let God have His way and not buck up against the process, He always finds a way to build up your mental and spiritual muscles in the process of one test, to make you resilient and sustainable in the next. God didn't want me to be lightweight in the ring. He didn't want me to be tossed to and fro whenever trouble tried to knock me down. God wanted me to be a heavyweight so the enemy's tactics would bounce off of me, and I could endure to the end.

Blessed is the man who remains steadfast under trial, for when he has stood the test, he will receive the crown of life, which God has promised to those who love him. —James 1:12

My pastor used to always say, "If you don't pass the test, you will end up having to repeat it." What did he mean by 'pass the test?' It took me a minute to understand this because growing up in church, I thought God wanted me to get everything right. It was heaven or hell, and there was a laundry list of things that I had to do to skip hell and get to heaven. And Lord knows I wasn't good at that. But what I learned about God as we bonded more and more in the process is that God was not looking for me to have all the right answers in the test. He wasn't keeping a list and checking it twice. He wasn't looking for my perfection, but He was looking for my progression.

He wouldn't tell me that my works are as filthy rags and have a glorified body waiting on me if I was supposed to be perfect on earth. God is all-knowing, all-seeing, all-powerful, and a realist. He knew the state of my heart and my intentions. He knew that I would mess up along the way like Abraham did, but He still blessed me and my seed. This is why I thank and praise God for His grace. The goal in passing the test was to find the answers to the life lessons. While I was in the fire, He wanted me to learn from the process, grow from the process, and acknowledge Him in the process. Those things right there are the correct answers to the test. If I could obtain those life lessons, I could use them to change my behavior, attitude, and outcomes.

We get so caught up in the things we're going through that we forget that God is our Father and wants us to be victorious. If you are transitioning, count it all joy. That means you're going from one level of anointing to another. You're evolving into something greater. In this transition process, you are like clay. God puts you on His potter's wheel and began to cultivate you. Initially the clay on the potter's wheel is unstable. It's wobbly, it's sloppy, and it takes the potter time to shape and mold you into what He desires for you to be. Hence, your growing pains, worry, doubt, and uncertainty. While you're on the wheel He's kneading, pushing, watering you, and raising you up. Hence, the sleepless nights, the tears you cry, the lashing out, and the poor choices you made. God was prepared for all of that. He already had a remedy. It's called mercy. The remarkable thing about God is He's not too big to meet us where we are in the process. He knows you are a whole person that encompasses many complexities and facets. He doesn't just embrace and show love to the parts of us that are more like Him, but He embraces and takes all of us as we are. "It is of the Lord's mercies that we are not consumed because His compassions fail not. They are new every morning: great is thy faithfulness." (Lamentations 3:22-23)

The Lord knew I needed His mercy going from two incomes to one. During that time, I was thinking, *how am I going to survive after such a drastic reduction in my household income*? I was worried, but God was not. He will bless you while He's molding you on that Potter's wheel and purifying you in the fiery furnace. He told me, *you're not going to survive, but you are going to thrive when it's all said and done.* God didn't want me to have just enough, He wanted me to have more than enough. He just wanted me to trust Him.

I learned in the process that you don't know God as Jehovah Jireh, your provider, until you are down to your last dime. You won't know Him as a heart fixer until your heart is broken. He knows the process hurts. He sees the tears coming down your face. He can feel your every emotion while you're going through it, but don't abandon the process. I know you didn't expect the fire to be so hot up under you, but God knew what He could get out of you if he turned up the heat. I thought the process of this transition was going to kill me, but God knew it was going to help somebody else to live.

Getting to know yourself in the process

I love that song by Kelly Clarkston, *"Stronger"* *(What doesn't kill you)*. One of the lines in the song says, "What doesn't kill you makes you stronger, Stand a little taller, and doesn't mean I'm lonely when I'm alone." Looking back over my trying transition, I used to resent the process that got me to where I am today because I thought it took me off my path. I know now that when you are being led by God, and you are in His will, you are always on your path even when it doesn't look like it or feel right. I've learned that the process is what makes the end result that much sweeter and your love for God that much stronger. It is in the process that makes you appreciate where you come from to get to where you're going. The difficulties of your transition is not fun, but it is necessary. The challenges that come with it are what we try to avoid, but God uses the good, the bad, and the ugly of the process to frame you into the best version of yourself. He takes every nuance of your story to cultivate your journey and navigate your path. God shakes things up in our lives, not to make us resent the world and the people in it, but to pull something out of us that He wouldn't necessarily get otherwise.

Like my Algebra teacher, God looks at the methods and the formulas of the route used to get us to our destination because He knows that the biggest lessons in life don't come out of the route with all the shortcuts and the least resistance. I understood "No pain, no gain" when it came down to going through the process of "looking the part," but I didn't understand it when it came down to going through the process of *being* the part. But while transitioning in my journey and finding my way through the unknown, God put a drive in me to be great and to do great things, and God challenged the greatness out of me.

Some days during the process, I felt like a weak, sensitive time bomb ready to explode at any time. Other days I felt small and insignificant wanting to crawl up under a rock and stay there. In the process, I felt an overwhelming feeling of emotion, and I had time to think about everything that transpired and what I wanted my destiny to look like. Proverbs 3:5-6 says, "Trust in the Lord with all thine heart; and lean not unto thine own understanding. In all thy ways acknowledge him, and he shall direct thy paths."

In my mind, the process was either going to make me or break me? But in God's mind, the process was going to prove me. God knows that everything is proven under pressure. It was going to prove that I was stronger than I thought I was, and I had more in me than I thought I had. The proof of who I was in God was in the process. Like Job, I can say, "though you slay me, yet will I trust him." God used my troubles to prove to the devil that I was true to it and not new to it. And when the devil saw that I wasn't turning my back on God, the heat got more and more intense in the furnace. I had to hold on to God a little tighter and learn how to trust Him even more. Some of the things I was going through didn't make any logical sense. It didn't look normal, it didn't sound normal, and I would wreck my brain trying to figure it out. But God didn't want me to figure it out. He didn't want me to worry about what the next person was doing or wasn't doing. He wanted me to put it in His hands and leave it there. He knew it didn't make sense to me, but it made perfect sense to Him. While I was worrying about things in my past, God had already worked out my future. He just wanted me to be present and stay the course, trusting the process was working for my good.

The enemy wants you to think that God doesn't love you because He allows you to suffer. The enemy wants you to believe that God abandoned you when He saw you crying your eyes out and didn't respond.

Peter 5:10 says, "And after you have suffered a little while, the God of all grace, who has called you to his eternal glory in Christ, will himself restore, confirm, strengthen, and establish you." The reason why He didn't come to save the day was that He desired to save your life. We are looking at a moment in time, and He's looking at how He's going to take that moment to change your life and someone else's. He knew "the sufferings of this present time are not worthy to be compared with the glory which shall be revealed in us."(Romans 8:18) This is the reason why God didn't respond right away. This is the reason why He didn't command His angels to relieve you from the pressure. He wanted you to be like the tree planted by the rivers of water, as the book of Psalms says. So, no matter what comes your way, you will not be moved. There were many times when I asked God to let this cup pass from me in so many words, but what He did instead was give me more grace to take the heat on the front end, so I could be more anointed and powerful on the back end. I didn't know who I was until I was tested and tried. It was only until going through the fire and coming out stronger that I knew I was a threat to the enemy. The bet was that I wouldn't come out as pure gold but as damaged goods. But when I came out of the process pressin' pretty and living better than before, the enemy had to wonder what kind of dirt God made me with. *#keeppressinpretty*

CHAPTER 6

LOVE YOURSELF, HONEY!

My prayer for you: *I pray that you don't let those circumstances devalue the love you have for yourself.*

"Love yourself" is so cliché, and I know you hear it at every woman's conference or in every self-help book. And while I agree with this cliché and perpetuate the same message, I had to research what it truly meant to love myself. I had an assignment in counseling that introduced self-care to me, and it helped me love myself when I didn't feel lovable. I learned that for me, it was easier to love myself when I saw myself in a good light, but when it was time for me to love myself from a place of brokenness and despair, it was harder for me to do. This caused me to really take a deeper dive into what loving yourself actually means to me and looks like in real-time. I had to examine the root of where love started for me in order to get an understanding of how I viewed love for myself. My introduction to love started out with my parents. Not necessarily how they started out loving me, but how I saw them love each other. Then it transferred into them loving me. They were my first examples of what love looked like. While they were raising me, "love" was rarely vocalized. I didn't hear "I love you." It was more so actualized through them taking care of me and giving me the things I needed. I love my family and friends, but I didn't know how to verbalize it or show affection. We weren't a huggy, kissy type of family, but I knew that my family loved me; they just showed it in a different way. When my parents separated, I was extremely sad and traumatized. I didn't understand why my family had to be apart. As a child, you don't look at your family dysfunctions as seriously as the adults do. You just look at it as normal family stuff. At the time, I just wanted what I always knew to be true; and that was mom, dad, and my siblings to be together. After the separation, my feelings of hurt, anxiety, and emptiness were never addressed. The thought of counseling was nonexistent in my community because of a lack of education and awareness. Back in those days, with no social media or a quick search on google, divorce was not discussed with children. Children were to stay in their place and not talk about grown people's business. If you're black, you know firsthand, or you've witnessed someone being told to "be strong," "get over it," or "life is not fair, that's just the way it is."

In my case, things were just not discussed, so the dismissing of my feelings as a child didn't allow me to love myself properly as an adult. I went on with my life and had to work through and internalize my feelings and emotions privately and alone. It was almost like business as usual, and I went on with being a kid. I later learned that everything that I knew about loving myself properly came from how my feelings were disregarded after the breakdown of my family structure as a child. That experience built a strong wall around me. My compassion level for myself was low in terms of acknowledging and dealing with my feelings. I considered myself strong, and feelings were not important in the grand scheme of things. So, loving myself was correlated with how I perceived myself and what I thought I deserved.

When you look back over your life, what was your introduction to love, and how does that affect how you love yourself? In order to give yourself love, there has to be love deposited in you that you can withdraw from. Some of you are starting from a deficit. You can't make a withdrawal because nothing has ever been deposited. Maybe you haven't been shown real love to know what it looks like for yourself. Maybe the love you were shown was based on the conditions of what someone could get from you. Maybe you've experienced some type of abuse, and you think that somehow it was your fault, so now you don't deserve to be loved. Everybody has a different concept of what love is, and depending on your experience of love, that will determine how you define love for yourself. I had to compare my definition to what my creator says about love. 1st Corinthians 13:4-7 gives a clear definition of what love is. This gave me a good starting point on how to properly love myself and others. It says, "Love is patient; love is kind. It does not envy, it does not boast, it is not proud. It does not dishonor others, it is not self-seeking, it is not easily angered, and it keeps no record of wrongs. Love does not delight in evil but rejoices with the truth. It always protects, always trusts always hopes, and always perseveres." When I read this scripture about love, I was enlightened to the fact that love is not love unless it's tested, and love can only be demonstrated through action. It's not about feeling goosebumps or hearing a bunch of things that tickle our ears. It's not about good sex or falling for someone. God laid the blueprint on how to love. He showed us that love is not a feeling, but it is something that you will yourself to give. Feelings are fickle. You can feel one way today and another way tomorrow. He doesn't choose to love us only when we're doing our best for Him, and we're obeying every commandment. He loves us when we are cutting up and acting a fool, because He doesn't see us as the mistakes we make. He knows that love is a call to action, and a decision made when the circumstances and people are not agreeable. He loves us based on the facts of who He is and not on the facts of who we are. He knows that we are wretches undone, and our works are as filthy rags, but He loves us unconditionally. So, if He can love me despite my flaws, then that gives me permission to love myself with flaws and all. But the question still remains, how do I do that?

Now that I have entered into a new chapter in my life, what does loving myself look like in real-time? How do I love myself every day while transitioning out of something that left me feeling so unacceptable? Growing up the way I did, I always thought that loving myself was all about getting Mani's and Pedi's, taking myself shopping, treating myself to a good lobster dinner, traveling, and just spoiling myself with material things. After learning so many valuable lessons in my transition, I start to realize that loving myself doesn't start with transactions but starts with planting seeds. I was trying to love myself from the outside in, but I was most fulfilled when loving myself from the inside out. I had to course correct where I put my energy. All the energy we put in being mad at somebody or focusing on the bad things that happened in our past need to be repurposed to investing in ourselves. All the external things and treats are great and have their place, but I had to start planting seeds of hope, acceptance, forgiveness, and courage into my heart and mind to have a long-lasting sense of fulfillment. I had to love myself enough to get the help I needed for the things that weren't acknowledged in my childhood. I had to tear down the walls I built around my insecurities as a way of guarding my feelings. This way, I didn't have to deal with my emotions because they didn't matter anyway. I learned how to love myself broken, which gave me a new appreciation for loving myself healed and whole. Therapy made me deal with my feelings and care for myself mentally and emotionally. Like anything else worth doing, loving yourself was a process, and it requires a sense of balance and emotional intelligence. The seeds I planted in myself through the grace of God produced something that others can prosper from. When you love yourself, you can properly love others.

Here are three seeds of self-love God planted in my life that I hope to be beneficial to you on your journey:

1. **Choosing myself over compromising my-self**: There is a great quote that says, "If you don't stand for something, you will fall for anything." Loving myself meant that I had to re-establish my set of values for my newly single life. I had been so far removed from the dating scene that before I went out dating and sharing myself with people, I wanted to take some time to figure out

what I wanted. I had to get to know myself all over again. I had to reassess my life and find out what makes me happy so I wouldn't be relying on someone else for it. Many times, we're anxious to get out into the dating scene looking for love to fill a void that was left in us from our past relationship. As a result, we're disappointed and frustrated when we don't get the love, we were supposed to give ourselves in the first place. We don't want to find ourselves in situations where we are drawn to people who need saving or have unresolved traumas that we end up carrying as well as the unresolved traumas we have in our own lives. Sometimes as women, for some reason, we feel it's our job to rescue people when we need God to rescue us. I am not looking for a trauma bond to make me feel good about myself. I don't want to be drawn to someone's pain, but I rather gravitate to someone's purpose. This meant I had to have a standard and use the morals and values of that standard as my compass to discern what is in my best interest and connects to my purpose. This meant that I had to start thinking more with my head than with my heart. The heart is nice, but it can get you in trouble. I could no longer make emotional decisions for things that required logic and common sense. I desired to be a better woman in this new chapter and beyond. Therefore, I had to set an expectation for myself that was grounded in a set of principles that allowed me the freedom to choose myself over anybody or anything that compromised what I stood for and who I represented. I made the decision to choose myself before compromising myself for the sake of not being alone.

2. **Choosing a healthier lifestyle:** What I love about God is that He deals with the whole person and not just the spiritual side of us. He realized that too much of anything can be a bad thing in the grand scheme of things. Even He's not too heavenly bound that He's no earthly good. III

John 1:2 says, "Beloved, I wish above all things that thou may prosper and be in health, even as thy soul prosper." God wants to make sure that our mind, body, and soul is flourishing as well as our bank accounts. (God don't want no broke Saints, but I digress. That's a topic for another day.)

It would have been easy to let myself go after my transition, but that goes against the "Keep Pressin' Pretty motto. So, taking care of my mind, body and soul was the quintessential way to love myself. Taking care of my **spirit/soul** was important because the soul is where my moral compass is housed. It is where my values and principles live. The person governing your soul determines the fruits of your spirit. Therefore, I took care of my **mind** (mental health) by doing my best in letting any and everything go that was trying to take me out through stress and anxiety. I had to strengthen my mind by using my faith to combat the tricks the enemy would try and use against it. Your mind is like a computer or a USB flash drive. The more you download, the more you can recall, and that's why I began downloading positivity and words of inspiration into my psyche. We have to safeguard our minds and spirit daily. I had to stay away from certain things, music, and people that carry a negative evil vibration that could potentially bring my spirit down. Certain things are draining and corrupt to your mind and spirit, and it leaves you empty or full of self-defeating thoughts.

Peace was the key element to my mental health. It was something I had to intentionally protect. Philippians 4:6-7 says, "Be anxious for nothing, but in everything by prayer and supplication, with thanksgiving, let your requests be made known to God; and the peace of God, which surpasses all understanding, will guard your hearts and minds through Christ Jesus." Happiness is my choice, joy is my strength, and peace is my gift. Like the church mothers used to say, "The world didn't

give it to me, and the world can't take it away."
I could no longer let my situation get the best of
my mind. I needed all my mind for where I was
going. I had to be at peace with what happened
or didn't happen in my life. I had to follow the
serenity prayer so my mind would be at ease. God
said this is what loving yourself looks like.

Lastly, it was so important that I took care of my
body. God gave us one body and one life to live,
so why not treat it with respect and love, right?
I had to remember that after going through my
transition and dealing with bouts of depression.
I was raised in a black family from the south, and
we fixed everything by eating good food. Some
of you know what I'm talking about. Smothered
ribs, ham hocks, pork chops, food cooked in
lard, and all things carbs. So based on the way I
was raised, I would be comforted for sure, but I
had to consider my waistline, and not try to fill
my void with food. I had to look at food for what
it was, and that is a means to nourishment. I'm

learning how to eat to live and not live to eat. We have to be realistic with ourselves when it comes down to our physical health. I know God is tired of hearing his people say, "Heal my high cholesterol Lord or lower my blood pressure, Jesus," but we are quick to buy a fried chicken dinner from the church after service. We are quick to go to an all-you-can-eat restaurant and try to eat for a whole week in one sitting. Just sayin'. I'm not pointing fingers at anyone but myself because I know none of you reading this book has done that. God dealt with me about taking responsibility for my overall health and not using Him as the catch-all for my bad choices. He wants us to love ourselves enough to not make choices that will compromise our health and give us diseases. The mindful decision to change my eating habits and exercise more was due to me being diagnosed with high blood pressure. And even though I believe God for my healing, I had to meet Him halfway with my free will.

3. **Choosing and letting go carefully:** I believe you are the company that you keep. Loving myself meant I had to choose good people that wanted to bring the good out of me during a bad time in my life. You need to have people who truly love you in your life, not only in the good times but in the bad times. I'm grateful to have family and a small group of friends that helped me pre- and post-divorce. They contributed to my growth, my peace, and my overall well-being. I chose very carefully who I wanted to divulge information to because I only wanted people who had my back for real and would tell me the truth no matter what. You need a balanced and well-rounded perspective when choosing the people to engage during a crisis. I needed people I could disagree with, and they weren't quick to cancel me or gossip about me to others. I didn't want "yes" people around me because at certain times during the battle, I wasn't in my sound mind. I wanted individuals around me

who challenged me with their conversations, celebrated me during my victories, and loved me through my adversity. I needed some friends that weren't too proud to pray and give me wise and sound advice. You don't need folks in your life that's going to encourage you to slash tires and key cars. Love yourself enough to stay out of jail or away from people giving you advice on how to get there. You can't be afraid to let people go and sincerely wish them the best, because like the old saying goes, there are people in your life for a season, a reason, or a lifetime. I learned that loving myself meant taking inventory of my life and being willing to purge things and those who are not conducive to my growth and purpose. Everybody can't go where God is leading you, because they won't understand the assignment, and that's okay. What God has for you, it is for you, and your real friends will understand because they have their own purpose. ***#keep-pressinpretty***

CHAPTER 7

KNOW YOUR WORTH

My prayer for you: I pray that you know that you are worth every good thing that God has for you.

Naturally, in the process of divorce and post-divorce, you acquire some insecurities along the way. The enemy will try to get in your head and make you feel like you're the less than and you're not worthy of being loved. He has no compassion about what you're going through, and he wants you to feel worthless. I experienced all of these feelings and more when working towards my healing. With no precedence of what feelings to expect during this process, unbeknown to me, it would open up Pandora's Box that contained suppressed feelings I had concealed for years. It exposed things, including old scars that either hadn't been reconciled or hadn't been revealed. When I looked inside the "Pandora's Box," I was confronted by the insecurities of a little dark chocolate nine-year-old girl feeling unworthy. Like so many little girls with dark melanin, I remember thinking that my dark skin was not good enough. Even after closing Pandora's Box and refusing to deal with what was inside of it, I found myself still trying to reassure my nine-year-old self while maneuvering through the issues I had as a full-grown woman. I had to tell her that she was not pretty for a dark skin girl, but was pretty because of her gorgeous dark skin. I had to give her the validation she was always looking for from the first man she ever loved. Colorism was something that was known in the black community, and some complexions appeared to be more favorable than others. For years, even after I got married and had a child, I didn't feel like I measured up. I allowed society to deepen those insecurities by projecting their standard of beauty upon me. I based my worth on what wasn't said to me by my father instead of basing my worth on what my Heavenly Father created me to be. I had to reconcile with the little nine-year-old girl I left behind and never built up, so she could appreciate the potency in the rich, beautiful skin she was in. I don't blame my father for not re-assuring me, but the little chocolate girl inside of me wanted me to confess what I needed God to address and bless in my life.

Many of our insecurities have been hidden for years, and all it would take is the right tribulation to bring out what we have put away in the back of our minds for so long. We wonder why we doubt ourselves and think we can't do certain things in life, not understanding that what we thought was hidden away in our minds is actually the backdrop to our daily lives. We subconsciously stand in front of those insecurities and anxieties all the time when making choices for ourselves. It's time to reveal what you want God to heal. Somebody made you feel like you weren't worthy. Somebody told you that you weren't good enough. Or maybe that somebody was you. The enemy can play on our emotions and intelligence and make us think things about ourselves that are totally untrue and go against our Creator. This is why II Corinthians 10:5 says, "Casting down imaginations, and every high thing that exalteth itself against the knowledge of God and bringing into captivity every thought to the obedience of Christ." The enemy will have you believing that you need something from somebody else to make you happy about yourself. The irony of this is, God never needed anyone to validate what He created and breathed life into. The last I checked, God didn't get anyone's approval when He divided the light from darkness, put the sun and the moon in its place, and made man in His image after putting the finishing touches on the heavens and the earth. Our God is so excellent that He went as far as complimenting Himself, and said what He created was good. To make things even more interesting, God loved His creation so much that

He thought it would be fitting to have an insurance policy in the beginning by way of His only begotten Son, Jesus. Seeing as though He is the Alpha and the Omega, the Beginning, and the End; He knew that His creation had free will and a weakness that could destroy everything He designed if He didn't have the second Adam in mind. Jesus not only redeemed the world back to Himself, but He made what was once an unworthy creation through sin, worthy again by the shedding of his blood. We went from being His creation to now being His children. Therefore, you and I didn't just become worthy; we were *always* worthy. You were worthy before the foundation of the world. Your worth is not determined based on the skin you are in or the mistakes and good deeds you would do over your lifetime. He determined your worth based on His unconditional love and sovereignty. When God decreed and predestined you as His child, He had no ulterior motives, and it could not return unto Him void. God knew you wouldn't have all the answers; He knew that you would be born on the wrong side of the tracks, He knew that you would fall short of His glory, but God thought you were worthy enough to save. He thought you were worthy enough to love. He thought you were precious enough to die for and worthy enough to forgive. So don't base your worth on how you feel or how someone feels about you. You have the authority to say, "For it was you who created my inward parts; you knit me together in my mother's womb. I will praise you because I have been fearfully and wonderfully made." (Psalms 139: 13-14)

Tears welled up in my eyes when I thought about this fact. I read that scripture, and I remember when I was at my lowest point, and I was curled up in a fetal position in the corner of my room, wrestling with all my insecurities and feelings of unworthiness. God put a battery in my back using that scripture. He helped me see things differently and walk in confidence. I had an incredible thought of God creating me with Himself in mind. He knew me and designed me in His image and His likeness. He covered me in all my beautiful dark melanin for the world to see, and gave me the extra melanin protection against the damage from the sun's UV light. So, in all actuality, my dark melanin was always a part of my strength. Once I took the time to educate myself about myself, I was able to appreciate myself better. The enemy could no longer use what I thought was a weakness against me. Now my nine-year-old self was walking confidently as a beautiful dark skin woman. I am no longer stuck as a nine-year-old little girl with feelings of unworthiness.

Are you dealing with something from your past that makes you feel unworthy? Do you miss out on opportunities because you don't think you're good enough to have them? God wants you to know your worth, so the people in your life will know your value. I told you that God made you worthy, but the question is, do you believe it? I had heard "you are worth it" over and over again, but it was only until I believed it that it meant something. I had to look beyond my circumstances, stop feeling sorry for myself, heal what was broken, and believe God's word in order to start walking in my worth. I'm reminded of my favorite book about a woman named Ruth. Ruth was a baaaaad (in a good way) sista hunni. She refused to be left behind after her husband and two sons died. She followed her mother-in-law, Naomi, to a land that was not of her origin or religion. After the devastation of her tremendous loss, she could have stayed back in her hometown and had a pity party with her homegirls, but she looked beyond her loss and sought out new beginnings. I encourage you to take a page out of Ruth's book. Ruth entered into this foreign land with her mother-in-law and found her a hustle. She knew that what she wanted was going to take more than just a prayer; but it was going to take a hustle. She was gleaning behind these reapers hoping she would find favor and they would drop a little for her. She just so happens to be in a very rich man's field by the name of Boaz. How many of you are still looking for your Boaz? Keep following this story and take out your notepad.

There were so many heartfelt moments when I read the book of Ruth, but what fascinated me the most about her story is that Ruth didn't let her past dictate her future. She was gleaning for two days before Boaz laid eyes on her. In my mind, her hair was sweated out, her clothes were unkempt, and on top of that, she wasn't even an Israelite. Yet, she was hustling like she belonged there, and she had keys to the city. Boaz told her, "Listen to me, do not go to any other field, but stay here with my young women. No one shall harm you, and when you are thirsty, go and drink at our vessels of water." That piqued my interest when I read what Boaz said to her. Why do you think he gravitated to her in such a favorable way like that? After losing her husband and her sons, I could imagine her still mourning, but instead of having a 'woe is me' disposition, she was working and handling her business when he saw her worth.

Later he said to the reapers, "When you are reaping, leave some of the sheaves for her (Ruth); and drop out some sheaves from the bundles, where she may gather them." He saw her drive and tenacity even though she wasn't on his payroll. Which made him want to go over and beyond for her. To make this long story short, Ruth went back to her mother-in-law grinning and cheesing like us ladies do when we see a fine man. She had told her whose fields she was gleaning in and the favor she was getting from this handsome, rich man Boaz. Naomi, being the OG in the game, told her what to do and how to do it, and Ruth obeyed her mother-in-law and got CUTE. She went and put on her *"red dress and slipped on her high heels and some of that sweet perfume."* Just kidding, I don't know what she wore, but My, My, My by Johnny Gill came to my mind, and it fits the scenario perfectly. I digress....getting back to Ruth. She went to Boaz looking and smelling good and prayed over his feet, and the next thing you know, he made her his wife. Go and read the story of Ruth for yourself. I can imagine she didn't go to Boaz looking like a damaged widow, looking for sympathy, but she went to him looking like a worthy woman that was ready and willing to be his wife. You may ask yourself, what is the moral of the story, or what does this have to do with me? I'm glad you asked. Ruth knew her WORTH!! She knew she was worthy of love and happiness. Just because you experience loss doesn't mean you don't deserve to win. Although she had lost her husband and her children, she didn't let that horrible situation diminish her value. Yes, it was painful and heartbreaking, but she had to press past how she felt and follow her mother-in-law and continue to live. Maybe you are at a crossroad in your life, and you're wondering if you should stay behind or if you should move forward. Maybe you're transitioning out of your relationship, and you feel diminished and figure no one is going to see your value. I'm here to tell you when you see your worth, others will see it too. Ruth felt worthy of being in those fields gleaning grain. She didn't let the fact of her being a widow or not being an Israelite make her feel unworthy of the blessing that was before her. She didn't let fear stop her hustle and getting the man of her dreams. I believe God has something great in the works for you and me. We just have to know we're worthy to receive it. *#keeppressinpretty*

CHAPTER 8

MY SELF-ESTEEM BELONGS TO ME

My prayer for you: *I pray that you learn to build yourself and not wait on anyone to do what only God can do.*

Have you ever been so down and out that you, your 'SELF,' tried to do different things to help your ESTEEM? Before you roll your eyes and turn the page, just listen to how this could happen. Your 'SELF' was getting so low in the relationship with ESTEEM that it was looking for things to give it a boost. 'SELF' decided to take a break from your ESTEEM and do its own thing in hopes of boosting

ESTEEM. 'SELF' was getting in shallow pacifying relationships that lacked substance, trying to help ESTEEM, but ESTEEM was getting lower and lower. 'SELF' started smoking weed and just knew ESTEEM would enjoy getting high as a kite, but ESTEEM didn't get any higher, but was always hungry. 'SELF' would try to drink ESTEEM to a happy place, but ESTEEM was only getting more miserable. 'SELF' was shopping for new clothes every week, just so ESTEEM could look good, but underneath the Fendi and Gucci, ESTEEM was still broken. 'SELF' was looking for validation and happiness from her new baller boyfriend and just knew ESTEEM would get a kick out of him, but ESTEEM suffered and suffered. 'SELF' had the nerve to tear down someone else's esteem, thinking that her ESTEEM would feel better, but it only lowered ESTEEM even more. After all the attempts 'SELF' made to boost ESTEEM, she realized that her ESTEEM was not only getting more and more depressed, but 'SELF' was being degraded. 'SELF' needed ESTEEM to be motivated, validated, and inspired. She just didn't look within to find what she was looking for. 'SELF' had always looked for things outside of herself to boost her ESTEEM, but those things could only take her so far and only do so much. What do you think 'SELF' should do for ESTEEM?

I know the above scenario may appear to be in riddle form and seems trivial but, in this part of my transition this was me. I had to figure out and understand what was going on with my self-esteem. The enemy works through insecurities and weaknesses that cause you to regress instead of progress. The goal is to keep our self-esteem intact and strong. According to the Merriman-Webster dictionary, Self-esteem is a feeling of having respect for yourself and your abilities. So, self-esteem is important during your time of recovery because it determines how you feel about yourself and what you think you deserve. It sets the tone on what you will get and how far you will go.

After transitioning from such a traumatic

chapter of my life, my esteem took a dive. This is understandable. I was still dealing with the aftermath of all the things I suffered, and I questioned my ability to move forward successfully. You're going to have some days of feeling vulnerable and unconfident. You're going to have some days when shame and guilt creep up on you out of nowhere. It is okay. You are human, and it's okay to acknowledge those feelings. It's okay to cry and be irritated, but it's important to know how to recover from all those feelings. You can acknowledge them, but you don't want to give them all of your time. There are 3 lessons I learned about my self-esteem that help me navigate through my feelings about myself.

1. I had to be real about the fact that my self-esteem belonged to me. I am the person in charge of my self-esteem. I have to be the one responsible for keeping it healthy and high. I know we are not taught this in school, because nowadays everybody gets a participation trophy even if they lost,

but no one is responsible for how you feel about yourself, but you. Therefore, you have to do the work in building your self-esteem daily. The perception you have about yourself has to be greater and more important than the perception others have about you. And although you are in charge of your self-esteem, God is the Master of it. It is important that your self-esteem is connected to the Creator. He has the owner's manual for your self-esteem. If you believe what God says about you, then you will believe in yourself. Once you know who you are and who you belong to, you can be having a bad day or a bad week, but you will know that your esteem is not substantiated by circumstances but predicated on who you are in God. Isaiah 26:3 says, "Thou will keep him in perfect peace, whose mind is stayed on thee: because he trusted in thee." It's so important that we trust God and His word as it pertains to who He made us to be. God has made each of us with so many different gifts, talents, and capabilities that we should have no reason to look outside ourselves for what God had placed in us. Mental health has been a hot top lately and is a new phenomenon for communities of color. If you are having a hard time elevating your self-esteem, seek a therapist to help you with methods and techniques. They can also help you get to the causes of why your self-esteem is so low.

2. Do you set expectations on other people to boost your self-esteem? I learned that if you give someone the power to raise your esteem, then you're giving them the power to lower it. When you give someone else the authority over your esteem, you will then view yourself through their eyes and not through your own. Your esteem will then be on this emotional rollercoaster ride that is being controlled by someone else instead of being empowered by you. "It is better to trust in the Lord than to put confidence in man." (Psalm 118:8) It's ok for people to motivate and encourage you, but at the end of the day, it's going to

be up to you to believe in yourself and keep your esteem affirmed.

3. Beware of false high self-esteem. This is a big one because you don't realize it's happening. It happens when you look for external objects and material things to boost your esteem. The way you feel about yourself has to be separate from what you have or don't have. Otherwise, you will think you don't deserve to be treated with respect or think you're valuable unless you have these external things. These superficial things are nice, and it feels good for a moment, but if you already don't feel good about yourself, then you will only have a false sense of importance by having these things. This can also be true when you see someone that may not have nice things, or they don't dress a certain way, and you think they don't deserve to be treated with respect because of how you perceive them. John 3:17-18 (NIV) says, "If anyone has material possessions and sees a brother or sister in need but has no

pity on them, how can the love of God be in that person? Dear children, let us not love with words or speech but with actions and in truth." I want to make sure that my perception of life, myself, and other people is not based on things that hold no value, but should be based on love and a pure heart. We have to boost our esteem with things that are edifying to our spirit. This is outside of all the designer labels, thousands in the bank, a bunch of friends, or even degrees behind our name. You have to know who you are with or without all those things because if you were stripped of all those things today, who would be left standing, or would you collapse?

These three lessons were helpful to the healing of my self-esteem during the process of this journey. It gave me a new perspective about myself and my esteem. You will not be perfect at doing these things all the time, but you can use them as a point of reference. It was important for me to not allow my self-esteem to be triggered or degraded. I had to be strong and self-assured for what I wanted to do in the new life I was creating while transcending from my old chapter. I do have days when I feel those negative thoughts creep into my head about myself, but here are some things I do to combat those thoughts. (Not necessarily all at once)

- I pray over myself.

- Only speak positive declarations over myself to empower my inner woman.

- Remind myself that "feelings are not facts."

- Help someone in need.

- Show gratitude. Thank God for the wonderful things he has done in my life.

It's hard for me to stay in a negative space about myself when I do these things regularly. It gets me back centered and on track.

For the uplifting and maintaining of healthy self-esteem, I would like for you to write down 10 empowering affirmations or scriptures to boost your self-esteem.

MY SELF-ESTEEM BELONGS TO ME

1. _____

   _____

2. _____

   _____

3. _____

   _____

4. _____

   _____

5. _____

   _____

6. _____

   _____

7. _____

   _____

8. _____

   _____

9. _____

   _____

10. _____

    _____

These affirmations need to be said several times a day to yourself. You want it to be so embedded in the fiber of your soul that you start becoming the very thing you speak. When you list your affirmations to speak over your life, speak boldly and use declarations instead of passive language. For example, "I will be successful, or I am more than a conquer." Passive language leaves room for doubt, and we are too fabulous for fear. *#keeppressinpretty*

CHAPTER 9

I'M A GROWN WOMAN GROWING

My prayer for you: I pray that God expands your territory and elevates your thinking.

Traveling this bumpy road of my transition has been a cycle of challenges and tests. I learned that life is the greatest school master you will ever have. It always requires you to press a little harder, overcome a little more, and rise above a little higher. Remember when we were young and couldn't wait to turn 18 to say we were grown? We wanted to do everything on our own and didn't want anyone telling us what to do. But no matter what age we are, God has a way of showing us we're still growing. We don't really know what growth is until we're knocked in the head by life. We think we are eating the meat and potatoes of God until He gives us another portion, and we can't stomach it. Hebrew 5:14 says, "But solid food is for the mature, for those who have their powers of discernment trained by constant practice to distinguish well from evil." Heaven knows I went from drinking the baby's milk to eating the meat and potatoes of God after the transition I went through. I knew I was eating at the adult table at the family cookout. I thought I was grown and mature before all of this, but God knew I had another level in me that had to be cultivated. He wasn't necessarily concerned about my height, weight, body mass index (BMI), or age in the natural sense, but He was concerned about my height and depth in Him in the spiritual sense. While going through life, we wonder why we have to be tested and put through the fire. Why do we have to suffer so much pain? Why do we have to carry the weight of something that we are not fully equipped to handle? But God has a way of proving that we are never too grown to have growing pains. Those pains are not for our physical growth, but they are for our mental and emotional growth. Challenges and adversity serve as our teachers. They rule with an iron fist, but the goal is for us to grow and be wiser than we were before. Some of us are grown, but our growth was gradual. We were doing everything adults do, but we were maturing at a child's pace.

After all the research you've done and all the time you put into perfecting your craft, now it's time to put it to the test. This will prove rather or not it's working or if you need to go back to the lab to improve it. This is what tests and trials do for us. God uses the test to measure our progress in Him. It shows whether or not we learned and grew or whether or not we folded and fell short. It tests rather or not we are becoming more like Him. The test is the growth detector. It finds out how far you've come and how far you have to go. I found out that you really don't know what God can do unless you've been tested. Test and trials draw you closer to God. It makes people call on Him when they normally wouldn't.

I didn't understand it while I was going through it, but now I get why God took me out of my comfort zone. He knew my growth was only going to happen if he put me in a position where I had to figure things out. He knocked the crutches from up under me and left me standing there with nothing to hold on to. He took away my familiarities, my home, and all the things I relied on. This made me have to be creative and think outside of the box. I had to make something good happen out of a bad situation. This experience stretched me and gave me depth. It made me more flexible about what God was doing in my life. The hotter the fire got, the more I felt the urgency to get things done. I got comfortable with being uncomfortable, and that's when God knew I was ready for this new chapter. He knew the strength He put inside of me, but I didn't know what I had inside of me until I was broken. The only way you know what's inside of a shell is when it's been cracked.

God extracted greatness out of me by allowing life to break me down. The goal going into this new chapter was to elevate to new levels, and that would not have happened without the test God designed for my growth.

I believe my growth has been essential to my environment, and the growth of my environment is essential to me. Once I grew and stepped out of my comfort zone, my environment did the same. The reason why your environment will grow and evolve is because your environment is a reflection of you. If you are not ready to grow with your environment, it will push you out of it. As long as I am productive and advancing, my environment will emulate that growth. If I am depositing things in myself to get a positive return, my environment will reap the benefits of that and be productive. Your growth was not just for you. Your growth is going to empower someone else to grow and get better. *#keeppressinpretty*

GROW

G- Is for **ground**. Have you evaluated the ground you stand on while in transition? When contractors see land to build upon, they don't see it for what it is, but they see the potential of what it can be. The most important thing they check is the foundation to see what it's made of in order to start the construction. In the process of growing and re-inventing myself, I had to observe the lay of the land I was standing on before I could rebuild. I was shattered and needed to be repaired, but God saw beyond my brokenness and focused on my foundation. He wanted to make sure that all the storms I weathered didn't dismantle my stability and the groundwork He laid down in my life. What was above ground could be replaced and restored, but the foundation I stood on determined the outcome of my rebuild. Life is not fair, and when trouble comes our way, it reveals rather we are standing on quicksand or something firm and sustainable. God wanted to ensure that what I was standing on was something He could sew into, so when he threw down seeds of instruction and wisdom, they penetrated, started roots, and could reap a harvest when He came looking for His return.

R-is for the root of everything in your life. There is a root to everything you're going through mentally, physically, and spiritually. Why do you put yourself in situations that will jeopardize your wellbeing? Check your roots. Why do you feel like you're not enough and worthy of love? Check your roots. Why do you have so much aggression and hostility? Check your roots. Why do you run away from your issues instead of facing them head-on to resolve them? Check your roots. Why do you hate the people who love you? Check your roots. Think about a plant. The root is the nourishment to the rest of the plant. If the root is damaged or injured, it causes the plant to weaken. The weakened plant may then begin to show decline symptoms such as lack of vigor and reduced growth. Our roots are what helps us survive and what our offspring are feeding off of.

Have you wondered why you or your family are not growing? Dig deep and introspectively to get to the root of your lack of growth. Roots can be repaired, and plants don't have to die. Examining your roots may take you back to something that happened in your childhood or be as recent as your last relationship. Whatever it is, I encourage you to dig up the root and examine the source of the issue.

O- is for open. Are you open to help or counsel? Has your situation made you so hard and rigid that God can't work with you? As trying as my situation was, I wanted to be open to all the lessons and blessings God had for me during this period of growth. Proverbs 1:5-7 says the following:

- **5** A wise man will hear and will increase learning, and a man of understanding shall attain unto wise counsels:

- **6** To understand a proverb, and the interpretation, the words of the wise, and their dark sayings.

- 7 The fear of the Lord is the beginning of knowledge: but fools despise wisdom and instruction.

Sometimes the harsh reality of our transitions makes us put up a wall of defense. We would rather suffer in silence, pretending like everything is fine. I get it; I understand closing yourself off and trying to figure things out on your own. But sometimes, by shutting out the world, you can shut out God. God sends us messages and blessings, and He uses people to do it. We pray and ask God for answers, but when He sends someone with it, we shut them down. We reject the message because of the messenger. It may not be what we want to hear, but it is what God knows we need. He wants you to grow, so He may send someone to plant a seed in your life one day, fertilize you the next day, water you, and then send sun rays the day after that. You never know how God may send a message to you, so it's important that you don't let your situation harden your heart and tighten your hand because there is nothing going out, and there's nothing coming in.

W- Is for work. Are you willing to do the work to grow? Did you think you wouldn't have to do anything, and it would just happen on its own? My pastor used to say back in the day, "You can play now and work hard later, or work hard now and play later" (RIH Bishop. Kenneth Hoke.) I learned that my growth is predicated on the work I put in. Gifts and talents will make room for you only if you put them to work.

I told myself that I never wanted to be like the trifling person who was given money by his master and didn't do anything with it in the book of Matthew 25:14-30, "parable of the talents." A master gave five talents to one of his servants, two talents to another servant, and one talent to the next servant. Do you remember that story? The person with the five talents immediately traded them and made five more, which gave him ten. The one who had two talents did the same and walked away with four. But the one who received the one talent went and dug in the ground and hid his master's money. When the master came to settle the accounts, the one who had received the five was able to tell his master he doubled his money. That person was told, "Well done, good and faithful servant." "You have been faithful over a little; I will set you over much." The same rang true for the person who had the two talents. But the trifling one who dug up the ground and hid his master's talent and only gave him back what he was given was cursed. His master responded and said, at least you could have put it in the bank, and when I came to collect, I could have earned interest, but your triflin' behind buried it. This person was cast out, and his money was given to the person with the ten talents. This was an example of how we treat God when we are not willing to do the work. God doesn't want you sitting around praying over everything and being super religious, and yet you are at the same place He left you ten years ago. You don't have anything but what He left you with. You haven't increased what He gave you or expanded your mind to obtain more. Once I got up off my soapbox and put in the work, I was able to double and triple what God gave me. Doors began to open, and He gave me favor amongst men. Then He put me over much more because He saw that He could trust me over a little. I promise you that if you meet God with a willing heart and hard work, He will expand your territory and bless you beyond your wildest dreams. ***#keeppressinpretty***

CHAPTER 10

LABELS, LIPSTICK & LONELINESS

My prayer for you: I pray that God clothes you in His love and validate you with His word.

While traveling this tedious journey, I learned a lot about myself. Some things were great and honorable, but some things not so much. You know how you go to the car dealership to get your car fixed for one thing, and the mechanic discovers several other things that need to be fixed too. That is what happened to me when I was going to the Lord for my healing about some things in my previous chapter. I went to God for one thing, and He started revealing some other stuff. Don't you love the way God works?

He will give you a two for one special. He allowed me to see myself like I'd never seen myself before while walking with Him during this process. I could not take everything about myself into this new chapter. In order for me to transcend and go to the next level in my life, I had to be real with myself. I had to purge some bad habits and behaviors. But before I could purge, I had to confess and pull up the roots of why the bad habits and behaviors were there in the first place.

Can you say 'hot mess express' in a cute dress? Yep, I can admit it; I was a mess. I'm not ashamed to say it because the truth set me free. Esthetically, I looked cleaner than the board of health in these streets. I looked like I had it all together. I had my family, a dog, a house, driving in a BMW truck, and working on my business. My makeup was poppin', my hair was always whipped, I always had the latest drip in my wardrobe, and when I walked into a room, I appeared to be strong and confident. I showed up, did a good job, and looked fabulous doing it. From the outside looking in, it would appear that I had very few problems. But my grandmother used to tell me that "Nothing is what it appears to be!" And boy, was she right.

After showing up with what appeared to be a fabulous exterior, I went home, took off my clothes and all the exterior esthetics just to suffer from my insecure, depressed, and lonely interior. Alcohol and drugs were never my go-to for problems that I had, but a sharp purse or pair of shoes was what soothed me and comforted my heart. I used shopping to medicate myself. You may ask yourself; how do you medicate with clothes, shoes, and accessories? Medication is any remedy used to make the pain go away and make you feel good for the moment, and that's what clothing and accessories did for me. This medication wasn't prescribed by a medical doctor, but it was prescribed by the fashion designers. Shopping was what I used to escape from how I really felt about myself and Baaaaabay!!! I was the queen of shopping. Hear me!! It was nothing like going shopping after being stressed out at work, before or after getting my nails done, after having a bad day or a good one. I could always find a reason to go shopping. Shopping was like sitting on a therapist's couch and pouring out my feelings. It was my release that gave me some relief and joy. I like to call it "retail therapy." Don't let a good sale be going on. I would feel myself floating through the store as I carefully went through racks looking for my next piece of happiness.

As a person with self-esteem issues, I was looking for something to take the spotlight off my insecurities. I can't tell you what you're dealing with or the remedy you use to mask it, but I can tell you don't try to run from it, become numb to it, or get high to escape it. At the end of the day, when it's all said and done, the things you were trying to escape are going to be there waiting for you. I am a big believer that if you look good, you feel good. And while that is true, it is a temporary pacifier if you haven't taken care of the internal issues that continue to manifest when the clothing is taken off or when you've gotten sober from the alcohol or drugs. It was over-indulgence for me. It was using clothing to not only cover up my body but to cover up the fragile, insecure parts of me.

My inner woman was dealing with things that my outer woman knew how to disguise. The world around me saw me "dressed to the nine's," but when I was dressed to the nine's looking in the mirror, I saw someone self-doubting and unhappy. It was easier to use my wardrobe and makeup to suppress my insecurities than to face those things head-on and work on them. At some point, I had to deal with my shame, depression, low self-esteem, and feelings of unworthiness. I had to deal with the colorism issues I had towards myself for years. The exterior was the mask to cover up all the things that I suffered with in private. I was shopping every week for the weekend to make sure I was fly. I was slaying for the fashion gods honey, while looking for a sense of validation I wished I would have received as a child. It took me some time to dig deep and do the work to realize this. I had to ask myself, was my external "slay" a reflection of my internal "slay?" The answer was no. The two didn't match at all. I was broken and depressed at times and didn't really know my value outside of my new outfit. I was operating from a place of brokenness and used material things to conceal the cracks. I put lipstick and labels on it, thinking I could trick myself into feeling better about myself, but at the end of the day, I was still in a lonely place. I was using clothing to heal it, but really it hid it. No one knew that the outfit was covering up things that I had suppressed for years.

I remember just going through the motions (like so many of us do) of living and trying to succeed in life that I didn't take the time to dig deep or introspectively. It was only after going through a traumatic situation that devastated my life that I realized the truth about myself. I had to be honest with myself and become more self-aware of who I was versus who I portrayed myself to be. Sometimes you think your priorities are together until God allows something to happen in your life to check what's most important. Sometimes God wants to use you in a mighty way, but He has to empty your cup in order to fill it up. The things that were in my cup were too murky for God to anoint and use. I quickly began to realize I needed to work on my inner woman so I could show up as my authentic self. This was not for me to show people what I had realized, but it was for me to be honest and true to myself and God. God worked on me from the inside out. God had to strip me down, to build me up. It took some time to peel back the layers and dig up the roots. And although this was necessary, this was one of the most difficult things I had to do. It wasn't easy seeing myself so raw and vulnerable. It was hard looking at my past and how it was controlling the behaviors of my present. I had been hiding and in denial for so long that I broke down and cried seeing myself so revealed. I had to shine a light on my own front porch and dig out my own weeds to get to the origin of my internal issues that were impacting my habits and behaviors. I had to figure out why I was doing the things I was doing.

Why did I have to have the things I was buying? Was it really for me, or? Only after confessing and confronting my mess was I able to clean up my mess and heal from the inside out. The tools I found along the way helped me to know that while all these labels are fabulous and nice to adorn yourself with, Gucci is not good medicine for shame, BCBG is not therapy for low self-esteem, and Prada is not going to cure the pain I had been suffering with secretly. Instead of putting the latest accessory on it, I started to do a lot of self-reflection and become more self-aware. Instead of putting lipstick on it, I had to do some soul searching and forgive myself and others.

Now, I don't want you to misinterpret what you just read. It wasn't that God didn't want me to present myself well in public or start looking unkept when I left my home. The clothing, shoes, accessories, and fancy hair were not the problem. It is absolutely nothing wrong with shopping and looking your very best. The clothing and the external ornaments were not giving me the issue I had. It was the insecurities and internal issues that were hiding underneath the clothing that needed a makeover. God wanted me to be transformed by the renewing of my mind and not by the labels I wore. He wanted me to be pleasing to him first and then an inspiration amongst men. Psalms 51:10 says, "Create in me a clean heart, O God; and renew a right spirit within me." God wanted my intentions and movtives to be right. He wanted me to operate in purpose and not vanity. Now I am very careful and mindful about what my triggers are. I am much more intentional and purposeful about how I shop and why I shop because it was time to level up.

#keeppressinpretty

CHAPTER 11

MIRROR MIRROR ON THE WALL

My prayer for you: *I pray that God shows you the best parts of yourself.*

During my time of transition, I had to reconcile with the woman I was leaving behind, to fully embrace the woman I was becoming. I'd come to terms that this new path was not a path towards my downfall, but it was my path to growth and something great. The end of a chapter does not mean closing the book and putting it on the shelf. It simply meant I had to turn the page and get in a position to either continue the same story or create a new one. That was all up to me. The only person I had control over was myself.

In this new chapter, I have full creative control over the story, and God is the director and executive producer. I don't have to worry about anyone editing out my storyline or misrepresenting me to the people. The good thing about the free will of God is you don't have to wait until a lane open's up for you, but you can create your own. God wanted to make sure I was successful on this new path, so He asked, "when you look in the mirror, who do you see?"

Now that I was fully immersed in my new chapter, there were some things I had to critique about myself from the inside out. The totality of who I am was not going to be defined by this moment of transition. God has given me the power to define my life moving forward and bring new meaning to my purpose. With this power comes the responsibility of being self-aware. When God told me to look in the mirror, I began to take a long and honest look at all of myself. I didn't ask if I was the fairest of them all. I didn't deflect from who I saw in the mirror and try to project onto someone else. God has put the spotlight on me. He wanted me to see all of me in order for me to see what I could be. When God is dealing with you, He doesn't make other people your excuse. He doesn't make other people your crutch or scapegoat. Although I went through a tumultuous divorce and lost more than you will ever know, I had to check myself and hold myself accountable for the things I could control. I had to ask myself, in what ways could I improve myself in order to be the best person I can be? This self-reflection was not about blame, but it was about looking within and being honest about who I saw in the mirror. The person looking back at me was not entitled to anything. I was the only person who owed myself. I owed it to myself to get educated, achieve my goals, build wealth and leave a legacy behind. I had to want the best for me before I accepted the best from anyone else.

James 1:22-24 — Do not merely listen to the word, and so deceive yourselves. Do what it says. Anyone who listens to the word but does not do what it says is like someone who looks at his face in a mirror and, after looking at himself, goes away and immediately forgets what he looks like.

I didn't want to have the same old attitude, have the same old conversations and live the same old life. I needed to leave any ideologies or mindset behind that was not going to serve my new purpose. During this process of introspection, I knew I had a lot more to do. I was tired of not living up to my full potential. I no longer wanted to miss opportunities and chances to level up because I wasn't willing to evolve. So many people are unwilling to change even though they want something different. The complacency of doing the same things the same way is more comfortable than stepping outside the box to get something new by doing something different. When I took that honest look in the mirror, I saw someone fighting fear. I fight fear religiously. Fear wanted me to be the same person that got the same things the same way. Fear gave me excuses and put mirages in my mind to make me believe I couldn't do something before I even tried. When God blesses us to get to the door of our destiny, we cannot be afraid to open it and walk through. 2 Timothy 1:7 says, "For God hath not given us the spirit of fear; but of power, and of love, and of a sound mind." I had to encourage the woman looking back at me in the mirror and reassure her that God is not going to expand you without equipping you. He is not going to take you where He can't keep you.

My blessing was predicated on me changing my mindset. The new person with so much potential looking back at me in the mirror wanted to be more intentional with God. I wanted what I gave to be more meaningful and my light to be more impactful. I was ready to fish and not have fish handed to me. Just surviving was not an option, but living life abundantly was the plan. The new me was getting prepared for higher levels and was no longer afraid of heights. No more reducing myself to make the people around me more comfortable about themselves.

I could not go into this new chapter with my head down and looking for handouts. I had to go into this new chapter fearless and bold, working hard to create something that I could be proud of, and God could get the glory from. And in order to do this, I had to work on the woman in my reflection.

Everyone ought to examine themselves before they eat of the bread and drink from the cup. For those who eat and drink without discerning the body of Christ, eat and drink judgment on themselves. —1 Corinthians 11:28-29, NIV

LOOKING BEYOND WHO YOU SEE

God asked me "who did I see when I looked in the mirror", but now He's asking, "Who do I want to see?" God doesn't see us for who we are on the surface, but He's always looking at who we're destined to be. God is a progressive God who doesn't define us by what's in the rearview, but He's always looking ahead, and that's the way He wants us to be. Look your new self in the mirror and declare that I won't be afraid to mess up; I won't be afraid of what people are going to say; I won't be afraid to try and then try again, because "Greater is he that is in me, than he that is in the world" (I John 4:4). God wants us to see ourselves the way He sees us. The person He sees is GREAT and full of promise.

Who you see in the mirror right now can't be compared to who you will see if you fight fear by doing the self-work and look beyond what you see on the surface. When you look in the mirror, you might see a short-order cook, but God wants you to see the Executive Chef. You may see a janitor, but God wants you to see someone with their own janitorial company. Dress for the position you want and not the position you have. If you want to be a manager, and you are in an entry-level position, start dressing like a manager, start being more professional, start carrying yourself like a leader and be ready for the doors to open. You will have companies pay for your education and create a position for you. (I'm a living witness of that happening.)

Now when I look in the mirror, I see someone who is blessed to be here in her right mind. I see someone who is walking in her greatness. I see someone comfortable in the skin she's in and ready to shine her light in dark places. My image is not the same image I left behind, but it's a new image that God has redefined. *#keeppressinpretty*

What are five things you see looking in the mirror? What are five things you want to see looking in the mirror of your destiny? Remember, the goal is to slay from the inside out.

1. _____

_____

_____

_____

_____

2. _____

_____

_____

_____

_____

3. _____

_____

_____

_____

_____

4. _____

_____

_____

_____

_____

5. _____

_____

_____

_____

_____

6. _____

_____

_____

_____

_____

7. _____

_____

_____

_____

8. _____

_____

_____

_____

_____

9. _____

_____

_____

_____

_____

10. _____

_____

_____

_____

_____

CHAPTER 12

MY SUPERPOWER

My prayer for you: I pray that you save yourself and others with your superpower.

This book doesn't show any indications that I'm perfect, I have all the answers, and I'm a biblical scholar, but what it does reveal is my superpower. No, I don't go around taking down bad guys or aspire to deactivate bombs or save cats out of trees, but what I have discovered about myself while trusting God is the devil is no match for us. When God and I come together as a team, we are better than Batman and Robin. I know you heavenly bound, bible ninjas are saying to yourself, "God doesn't need your help."

And you're right; I never said he did. That's why it is a privilege and honor that He chose me as His vessel to join Him in overpowering the enemy. When I understood I was not wrestling against flesh and blood, I had to approach the battle totally different. The gloves came off, and I had to put on the whole armor of God. The devil came armed and ready to steal, kill and destroy, and after training with God and building my confidence in Him, I was not going down without a fight. This was not a fight that I could pull everyone I knew into, but I had to be calculated and connected to the only person I knew who specialized in spiritual warfare. I needed someone who could instruct me on how to combat the forces that couldn't be seen with the natural eye.

At a point in my transition, the pain I felt was so permeating that it cut deep into my soul. I felt so tormented and scorned that I thought God was punishing me. Maybe I did something wrong in my past, and now I'm reaping what I sowed. I totally understood Job when he questioned God's fairness and justice. Like Job, the human side of me was breaking down bit by bit, and the spiritual side of me was fading in and out. Some days I felt present, and other days I felt like I was disappearing under the darkness of pain. And although the enemy appeared to be winning the battle, he didn't know who he was messing with. The enemy tried to use the pain I felt going through my transition as a weapon to terrorize and stop me from moving forward, but God had something up His sleeve.

John 14:12 says, "Verily, verily, I say unto you, He that believeth on me, the works that I do shall he do also; and greater works than these shall he do; because I go unto my Father." Do you realize that God has given us the power and authority to do what he did on this earth and more? As a result of God being in me and I in Him, I have been given not just power, but a superpower that can affect the world around me like He did. My superpower is the devil's kryptonite. It is a power that weakens his ability to keep me shackled to my past and crippled by pain. My pain only had vitality because I gave it the power to rule over me. I subconsciously let it dictate my decisions and call the shots in my life. However, I didn't realize how powerful I was until everything hit the fan, and it was either fight or flight. When I took my power back, I not only disarmed the enemy, but I had the courage and strength to do greater works as God said I would do. I no longer let the pain of my past affect how I moved in life. I had to take back control, and the only way I could do that, was to be unapologetic about what I'd been through. I had to own my past and use my pain as leverage. I could only do this through faith in God. Hebrews 11:1 says Faith is the substance of things hoped for, the evidence of things not seen." I held on to that scripture close to my heart because all that had kept me alive was my faith. The substance it refers to was the only thing that could possibly hold the weight of my situation and keep me sane in the process. While going through the healing process, I didn't realize that God was using my faith to unlock the evidence of the things not seen within me. He wanted the evidence of things not seen to be manifested in my life. I Corinthians 2:9-10 says, "But as it is written, Eye hath not seen, nor ear heard, neither have entered into the heart of man, the things which God hath prepared for them that love him. But God hath revealed them unto us by his Spirit: for the Spirit searches all things, yea, and the deep things of God." God knew I was ready to dive deeper and go stronger for this thing called life. God was birthing something inside of me that would soon be evident through my superpower. God desires for us to go to higher heights and deeper depths in Him, but we can't seize the moment if we allow our painful past to seize us. When I made up in my mind that I wanted to be free from the bondage of pain, God unlocked a superpower within me that I didn't know was being developed in my spirit. The superpower that was being birthed in me was being cultivated in the pain I suffered. Think about it, when a woman is giving birth, she has to push through the pain and not run from it. If she ran from the pain, she wouldn't bring forth the life inside of her. She is constantly being told to push because the gift she is waiting for is on the other side of the pain. My superpower was brought to life when I stopped resisting the pain and pressed towards it. When I faced it and owned it, I took the sting out of it, and that's when God revealed how the pain can work for me instead of working against me. I have the superpower to leverage my pain into something that serves my purpose. Baaabaayy!! God blew my mind and put the devil on his knees with this. The enemy could no longer use the pain against me because now I'm using it to work for me. God and I double-teamed the enemy with this. He reversed the curse of my pain when I obeyed His voice and used my pain to propel my purpose.

Listen, I'm not the only one with this superpower. I'm no more special than you are reading this book right now. God wants to manifest this superpower in all of us. It is discovered when you stand up to the enemy and be unashamed about your painful past and the things you've struggled with for years.

When you face it and own it, you take the power out of it. Then you can flip it into something that will help others recover from their pain. The more pain you flip into purpose, the more you are using your superpower to defeat the enemy at his own game. If he can't use our pain as a weapon against us, he won't prosper. As crazy and trifling as the devil is, he knows that we have new mercies every day and old things are passed away, and behold all things are become new (II Corinthians 5:17). His goal is to blind us to the mercies and keep us seeing the mess, so he can win the battle. But can somebody say, "NOT TODAY DEVIL." I no longer let pain rule me and influence my decisions. I am no longer triggered by the pain in my past. I can talk about it without being depressed and bitter. It's called DELIVERANCE! It's called SET FREE!!

Through God's grace, I was able to break free from the pain that was like chains around my neck, wrist, and ankles. Pain no longer dictates how I treat people. It doesn't make me fearful of trusting anymore. My superpower didn't let pain kill my dream, but it nurtured it. Who knew that all this time, my purpose was being defined and birthed by my pain? God was turning what was supposed to destroy me into something that would eventually save someone else's life. If your pain, guilt, and shame didn't take you out, then flip that baby around and use it to stand on the enemy's head; give God some glory and be a witness of what God can do with what was intended to kill you.

When God frees you from the pain, pain is going to beg you to stay because it is selfish in that way. It wants you to sulk and wallow in it for the rest of your life, but it doesn't have power unless you stick around and give it energy. I know pain's cousin shame is going to rear its ugly head, but don't worry about how people are going to look at you and judge, because your superpower can turn shame into a shout. I used to let the enemy kick my butt with shame, but now I have shifted the shame into a shout of praise on the devil's head for all the incredible things God has done and is doing in my life. I learned that when God releases you from pain, it isn't just for you, but it is for all the people you dragged down when the pain was dragging you. Pain doesn't just stop with you, but it is transferred from generation to generation if it's not dealt with and cut off at the neck. With that being said, it is a reason why you went through hell and back. It is a reason why it hurt the way it did. It is a reason why you had to stay in it for so long. The best of you is going to come from the worst of what you went through. Your emancipation from the pain that wouldn't allow you to give a genuine smile, or a liberating laugh will stop the tears from flowing and stop the anger from rising.

As my story unfolds, I now live on Peace Ct, between Joy Rd and Fearless Point in the Choose Happiness subdivision. I pass by Pain Street and Shame Ave with a smile on my face knowing I have the SUPERPOWER to not go down those roads again. I'm not saying that life is not going to present you with more painful moments because it will. I'm not saying that life will be a bed of roses, and you won't ever feel pain again. But I've decided to operate and live my life from a place of purpose and not pain. I am no longer being led by pain, but I'm being led by purpose. I don't have to live on Pain Street and set up shop because when I flipped it into purpose, I started giving pain over to the Pain Killer. The Pain Killer is also the one who said, "With man it is impossible, but not with God. For all things are possible with God." (Mark 10:27) So add a cape to the armor of God you walk around in because you have a superpower that can reverse the devil's curse on your life. I triple dog dare you to flip your troubles into triumphs, struggle into strategy, and perplexities into projects. Everything that the enemy throws your way, through God, you have the superpower to reverse it and use it for your good and God's glory. Your purpose is connected to God's plan, and when you live out your purpose, it's leading someone closer to theirs.

#keeppressinpretty

CHAPTER 13

HUSTLE PRETTY

My prayer for you: *I pray that God gives the desires of your heart and you the wisdom and knowledge on how to maintain them.*

Preparation

I remember during the process of my divorce; I was fearful and anxious about my future as a single woman. I was so used to operating as a unit for so many years that my singleness was so obscured in my mind. In the midst of everything going on, it was hard for me to gauge what I was going to do. God reminded me about my humble beginnings growing up in the ghettos of Detroit. Getting it out of the mud wasn't new to me. I remember government cheese, food stamps, and Goodwill boxes under the Christmas tree. I remember taking two and three buses to work and producing under pressure. God said if I brought you out of that, I could provide and secure you through this. I had to not only believe God was going to take care of me, but He told me to come up with a vision for myself going into this next chapter. The great saying goes, "If you don't plan, you plan to fail." Habakkuk 2:2 (AMP) says, then the Lord answered me and said, "Write the vision and engrave it plainly on tablets so that the one who reads it will run." I quickly learned while going through my transition that without a vision and a plan to execute that vision, I was settling for whatever life threw my way. I refuse to let someone else determine my outcome. I had to envision myself the way I wanted to see myself in the future and not let my present circumstances dictate my will to dream and my leap of faith.

When I read Habakkuk 2:2, it let me know that my vision needed to be written down so I would have a guide to follow. So, I started writing. This was my preparation time, so when it was time to produce, I would be ready. I wrote down a set of short-term and long-term goals, and as I reached them, I checked them off one by one and moved on to the next. I wrote down where I wanted to live and the things I wanted to do post-divorce. I wrote out a budget of how much money I wanted coming in and going out. I wrote things down in the order that I wanted them to happen in. I wanted to take this a step further and do a vision board. I wanted to see my request of God live and in color. I posted the furniture I wanted, picked out the rugs and drapes to match. I posted the trips I wanted to go on and the different things I wanted to accomplish. I remember going to open houses, looking at homes I couldn't necessarily afford, but I was giving God an idea of what I was dreaming about. I asked God to show me how to make my means match my dreams. God wanted me to believe in Him like I had never believed before. I believed that He could make the impossible possible.

I decided to hang my vision board up in my room so it would constantly be before me, and I could hold myself accountable to it. I gave my vision purpose and an assignment. I was very specific in prayer and on paper about the things I desired and needed for my next chapter. God is into the details. So many times, we give God generalizations and wonder why we get blessings in general. It's not that God doesn't know what you want, but He wants to know if you know what you want. It was important that I breathed life into my vision. I didn't want to hold my vision hostage and not give it legs to stand on. That meant I had to support my vision with a plan. My vision was the overseer of my goals, and my plan was the outline for my goals to meet the vision.

I was excited because I finally felt like I was moving in the right direction. I didn't feel like I was stuck, but I had faith that things were going to work out. When I was asking God for all the things I needed and wanted, God wanted to know if He could have something from me in return that He could connect to. The faith I had couldn't just stay in my heart and on paper, but it had to be demonstrated in order to be real. It was okay that I took my vision, goals, and plans to God and asked Him to bless it, but what He wanted me to connect to was my commitment. This would be a true indication of my faith. I had to step out of my own way by not giving myself excuses and procrastinating on the things that needed urgency. Sometimes we can be our own worst enemy. We like to talk about having haters, but we need to make sure we're not hating against ourselves. I was willing to give God what He wanted in order to make my dreams come true. Plus, I couldn't afford to be lazy or negligent. After all the things I had endured and lost along the way, I had no other choice but to bet on myself. I had to make it happen or it wasn't going to happen. This was going to require SACRIFICE and DISCIPLINE. I had to create some new habits and get rid of some old ones quick, fast, and in a hurry. I began working on my credit, starting from the lowest debt to the highest debt and made consistent on-time payments that were over the amount asked for. I wasn't playing! I saved every dime I had, besides food and bills. I paper bagged my lunch for work, and due to the pandemic, I didn't go out, so I guess that can be looked at as a blessing and a curse. I picked up an extra job after working my 9 to 5, and some nights I didn't eat dinner because I was so focused on the mission I forgot to eat. Keep in mind, I was doing all of this in the fiery furnace and in the thick of my situation. I remember driving to work with tears in my eyes many times, but before I went into my job, I wiped my tears, touched up my makeup, and went to work. While I was diligent and faithful in the things God told me to do, God was working behind the scenes blessing the seen and unseen. In the midst of everything I was dealing with, God gave me favor and blessed me with a new job. It was a substantial increase and just what I needed to not only help me accomplish my goals but also boost my confidence. God will prove Himself to you through signs and wonders like He did when He performed miracles in Capernaum. (Luke 4:40-41) He gave me favor while the situation was still unfavorable. God showed up and showed out, but it was still work to be done.

I realized that my vision would only be fulfilled if it was connected to my goals. I had to be like a sniper, looking through a sniper rifle and visualizing my target. My vision was the scope used to look at my goals. If you don't have a target or goals, then you are directing your vision aimlessly. The sniper scope not only gave me a good view of my goals, but also blocked out other things in my peripheral that would cause distractions. My vision and goals were more important than what someone was posting on Instagram or my favorite show on Netflix. My vision became more important than going to the mall, shopping for clothes and things that were not serving my vision. And those who know me know that I was serious as a heart attack about accomplishing my goals if I sacrificed shopping. Sometimes our vision gets clouded, and our goals disappear because of what we allow to get in the way. You have to have tunnel vision. With tunnel vision, you are not concerned about what people are saying or not saying or worried about who's doubting you or patting you on the back. I knew that in order to pull all of this off, I had to be unbothered by the outside world and really focused on what God told me to do.

God said...KEEP YOUR MOUTH SHUT. Some of the best advice I ever received came from my daughter at 14 years old. She said, "Move in silence." (*She always was a kid with an old soul.*) I had to remember that the shoes God gave me to walk in, does not fit everyone else. It is not wise to let people know what you and God have discussed until God says it's time. What God and I talked about regarding His plan for my life was not for others to grasp and believe, but it was for me. Sometimes it takes us a minute to process and believe what God is saying to us about us, so why would we think that someone else is going to be open and understanding to something that wasn't meant for them. Doubters are always waiting for you to fail, especially when you tell them about your plan, and something happens where it doesn't come to pass. This will only discourage you from moving forward and trying again. So that's why God said KEEP YOUR MOUTH SHUT.

Produce

The next step I had to tackle was producing results. It was time for me to put some things into action. Vision, plans, and goals are just that without execution. My plan of execution looked great on paper and in my mind, but I was contemplating how I was going to pull these things off in the midst of the infamous COVID-19 pandemic of 2020. You know what I had to do? I had to not find any excuses not to do it. Failure was not an option. After building my credit score, stacking my coins, and getting pre-approved, I contacted a realtor (can somebody say, REALTOR!!). It was time for me to get a home. I found a place and put down a good faith deposit. I paid for the inspection and the appraisal, and the deal fell through. I was disappointed, but what God had for me wasn't going to miss me. My blessing already had my name on it, I just had to find it, and so I looked again. The devil was so mad that I had the unmitigated gall to trust God for something that big after going through something so traumatic. He was in his feelings about me progressing and doing the things he told me I wouldn't be able to do. He tried everything in his power to stop me, but God was leading the charge. I went from being homeless, sleeping on somebody's couch, sleeping in a hotel for weeks, to having a DEED (in my name) to my own home. Can somebody shout, "WON'T HE DO IT!! While people were losing their jobs, homes, and businesses in 2020 (God bless them), I closed on my home in the midst of a pandemic and after a devastating divorce just a few months prior. OOOOOOWE! The enemy was mad. I didn't just transition into my new chapter, but I transcended like God promised. And to pour salt on the devil's wounds, the biggest long-term goal I put on my vision board was being an author, and here you are reading my book!!!

I'm a living witness that YOU CAN MAKE IT HAPPEN. You don't have to be the stereotypical story post-divorce. You don't have to be broke, busted, and disgusted. You don't have to live like a damsel in distress, waiting on the next man that's not promised to you. You can be everything you put your mind to and more. You can overcome and make a full recovery; I promise you can. Your drive and your determination have to be greater than your pain and suffering. Everything that the devil stole, God can compensate you with that and more. God is waiting on you to write the vision, so He can make it plain. He is waiting on you to make the appropriate sacrifices and put in the work so He can give you the desires of your heart. I know your vision is exciting, and your future is so bright, now execute the vision and produce results. I challenge you to hustle pretty and come up with a plan in the fiery furnace, so when the heat has subsided, and the dust has settled, you are ready to dominate your future. When you survive and make it through to your new chapter (which I know you will), your preparation is going to produce some amazing results.

I am going to give you an opportunity to write down your vision for yourself. Write down your goals (short & long term) and what behaviors will serve those goals. In addition to that, think about your plan of execution to make that vision come to life. Remember that your vision is your scope to slaying your goals. After you write them down, check off each one as you complete them until you've accomplished them all. I am so excited for you because when you check off that first goal, you are going to be more confident to check off the next. Don't give up on yourself! *#keeppressinpretty*

Vision:

_____

_____

_____

_____

_____

_____

_____

_____

_____

_____

Goals:

_____

_____

_____

_____

_____

_____

_____

_____

_____

_____

_____

_____

Behaviors that serve your goals:

_____

_____

_____

_____

_____

_____

_____

_____

_____

_____

_____

Plan of Execution:

_____

_____

_____

_____

_____

_____

_____

_____

_____

_____

_____

CHAPTER 14

THE SWEET AROMA OF VICTORY

My prayer for you: I pray that you walk in your victory.

Like the three Hebrew boys, I too, know how it feels to be in the midst of the fire, not knowing if I would ever get out alive. The fire was turned up to the highest degree because the plan was not just to see me burn but to strip me of everything and watch me lose my mind. At the time, I couldn't comprehend the loss, the pain, the heartache, or understand why it had to be me. The devil thought, "Another one bites the dust--she won't recover from this." According to the devil's calculations, I would be damaged goods and too broken for God to use as His vessel. He just knew that the fire was going to burn me to ruins and leave me destitute. He thought that my faith would disappear indefinitely, and I wouldn't have anything left in me to give. He wanted to silence me and muffle my voice. He thought that I would be so embarrassed by what happened that I wouldn't tell my testimony. My loss was the devil's gain. He loved seeing me confused and, on my knees, begging God to take the pain away. He laughed when he saw me depressed, angry, and barely holding on because he takes pleasure in our pain and devastation. He relished seeing me in the fire, but what he didn't see was God covering me, holding my hand, and being the other person in the fire with me.

Do you smell that? Can you smell that aroma in the air? That's the smell of VICTORY that emanates off of me after being in the fire. It's the sweet aroma that came from the fiery furnace when I walked out of it. The doors of the fiery furnace were finally opened, and I walked out with my clothes in tacked and with all my hair (the edges and grey hair is going to need treatment). I didn't smell like smoke and soot, but I smelled like VICTORY over depression, shame, guilt, and every other disparaging thing that was used to defeat me. After reading about Shadrach, Meshach, and Abednego, it was clear that the fire was never designed to burn them, but the fiery furnace was just the means that was used to incite praise from their enemy, Nebuchadnezzar. It was a demonstration of God's wondrous working power. God magnified Himself by making an example out of the three Hebrew boys, and He used the fiery furnace to do it. Did you know God was a show-off? God has already prepared blessings for your life to show you off before the enemy. When your life is not your own, and you belong to God, your fiery furnace experience will not be in vain. God finds a way to solidify Himself in the hearts and minds of man by making a miracle out of you. He has the power to use your life for His glory to affect someone else's story and set you up for victory. By no means was the victory my divorce (I wouldn't wish that on anybody), but the divorce was the means by which God used to draw me and others closer to Him. He used the worst of situations to bring out the best in me. The fiery furnace was predestined to make diamonds, and not ashes. God was able to find treasure in my tragedy. I was still valuable enough to give Him the glory. The enemy saw the fiery furnace as a means to finish me, but God used the fire to purify my thoughts about who I was and gave me clarity on who I wanted to be. I only saw where I stood in my journey, but God saw the beginning, the end, and everything in between. So, when I saw myself in a mess, stressed and depressed, He saw me as an author, advocate, and intercessor for those who are in transition and need to be empowered during their recovery. God set me up 'for real for real.' He had a plan all along that was bigger than me and greater than my circumstances. The enemy could not have predicted God using every lie that was told, everything that was lost, all the heartbreak and pain towards my victory. He could not fathom God using all of these things as a platform for me to stand on, to tell people how great God is. The victory was already won even before your transition. When you are walking with God, the game is rigged, and you are set up to win. God moves the goalpost until you cross the finish line. You are more victorious than you think. Psalms 23:5 says, "Thou preparest a table before me in the presence of mine enemies: thou anoints my head with oil; my cup runneth over." This scripture is a clear indication of vengeance that only God can give. This is why you shouldn't worry about fighting your own battles and making your enemies pay for what they did because God will repay. Don't worry about exalting yourself because when God exalt you, no one can bring you down. You have been anointed for this occasion, and your reward is going to be so great, it will have your enemies "clutching their pearls." *#keeppressinpretty*

VICTORS RISE UP

I declare and decree that I am not the devil's victim, but I am God's VICTOR. HAHAHAHA! I laugh because just over a year ago, I couldn't say that. I couldn't see my potential for seeing the problem. I thank God, I am no longer a victim of my circumstances, but I see myself as more than a conquer through Christ Jesus. The devil has no control over my mind or my heart because I am victorious! (Say it like you mean it.) I AM VICTORIOUS. Now claim it, declare it, and walk in it unapologetically. I have been through too much to not stand proud in my VICTORY. You are God's cream de la cream. You rose to the top when the odds were you falling to the bottom. You don't have to be ashamed of not walking in shame. You don't have to wear the scarlet letter and be embarrassed and ostracized about your painful past. SO, WHAT! Your situation is the topic of conversation. SO, WHAT! People don't know your side of the story but judge you based on lies. With victory comes peace. This is that type of peace that keeps you from going off on people, throwing blame back and forth, and worrying if people are looking at you funny because they think they know your business. As a VICTOR, you are FREE!! You are so free to live in your purpose and all the possibilities of your future that you are not interested in bashing men and degrading women to uplift yourself. You want to see everybody around you victorious. HATERS WHO? You are so focused on the lane God has created for you that you don't have time to recognize who your haters are. As a VICTOR, you know who you are and whose you are. You are not concerned about petty, insignificant things that are not conducive to your inner champion. When you walk as a VICTOR and not a victim, your spirit leaves a sweet and pleasant aroma in the air. The Lord replaced beauty for ashes; therefore, your spirit is radiant, and your aura is attractive. You're not bitter and carrying your past like suitcases, walking around asking people to help you carry those bags for you. Victors lay down their burdens at the altar, counselor's offices, and they "Keep Pressin' Pretty."

I realized that my past is just that—the past. I can't change it; I can't make it go away. All I can do is reference it to measure where I am right now, and because I choose to be great, my past doesn't stand a chance to my future. There is a song we used to sing in church that says, *"When I look back over my life, and I think things over, I can truly say that I've been blessed, I have a testimony."* As a VICTOR, I can now say, it is good for me that I have been afflicted; that I might learn thy statutes (Psalms 119:71). At the end of the day, I am truly thankful that God loved me unconditionally and was patient with me during my time of transition. I'm humbled that he allowed me to use my dark past to get somebody through to a brighter future. I hope after reading this book, you walk away feeling like you can accomplish your dreams and recover from your past because you are a VICTOR! ***#keeeppressinpretty***

KEEP PRESSIN' PRETTY: SLAY FROM THE INSIDE OUT PLEDGE OF COMMITMENT

Take this opportunity to be a part of the Keep Pressin' Pretty: Slay from the Inside Out Pledge of Commitment. Your garments are fabulous and chic, but is your heart and soul still broken and weak? When you look in the mirror all dressed up, do you still see a traumatized little girl looking back at you in your reflection? Does the person you see in the mirror truly represent the person you present to the world? Are you trying to cover up wounds that still hurt from your past? Sign your name and start examining your life from the inside out.

I _____ will make a commitment to God and myself to reveal and heal. I will no longer cover up my wounds and trauma with labels, makeup, drugs, alcohol, or sex. I promise to seek therapy to examine, heal and support my mental and emotional health, so I can slay from the inside out and not from the outside in.

Tag me on Instagram or Facebook @keeppressinpretty using the hashtag #slayfromtheinsideout, and I will share you on my Insta- stories!!

ACKNOWLEDGMENTS

In the Preface, which focused on using my testimony and experiences to inspire and encourage others to overcome in recovery, I recognized and empathized with you, the reader. You are my inspiration for writing my story and putting my truth on paper. God has blessed me to be a blessing, and I hope you can find treasure in your tragedy like I found in mine. So, thank you for taking the time out of your schedule to read this book.

We know it takes a village to raise a child, and although that child grows up into an adult, that village is still necessary for the support and covering. I would like to say thank you, Auntie Regina, for being my advisor and coach during the process of my transition. Some days

I don't know what I would have done without your counsel. Thank you, Granny, for letting me sleep on your couch when I needed somewhere to lay my head. Thank you, mom, for being a listening ear and an example of grace under fire. To my siblings, Chris, Isaiah, Jason, and Jasmine, thank you for having my back. To my group of girlfriends who inspired me, prayed for me, challenged me, and ministered to me along the way. Thank you all for encouraging me to Keep Pressin' Pretty!

ABOUT THE AUTHOR

Kisha Prince comes from very humble beginnings, but through the grace of God and hard work she has been able to pursue her dreams and walk in her purpose. She went from growing up on public assistance in the ghettos of Detroit, Michigan to becoming a college graduate, personal stylist, motivational speaker and divorce coach after healing from her own divorce. She was able to make sweet lemonade out of the lemons she was given on her journey.

Kisha started saying Keep Pressin' Pretty as an affirmation to herself and then turned it into a fashion blog and styling service. Keep Pressin' Pretty has grown to become a source of support and inspiration for women to encourage and heal themselves after trauma to restore their mental health. Kisha is on a mission to helping women reinvent themselves from the inside out. She is always on a quest for peace, joy, happiness, and finding ways to empower herself and others. She can be found on Instagram talking about healing and restoring her inner woman, while slaying and looking fabulous with her style and fashion.

Kisha enjoys writing, traveling, relaxing by the water, shopping, watching movies, and hanging out with friends and family. Out of everything she has done in her life, she is most proud of being a mom to a beautiful daughter.

Kisha would love to hear from you! Connect with her at keeppressinpretty.com or chat with her on Instagram and Facebook @keeppressinpretty.

Made in the USA
Columbia, SC
21 December 2021

51299627R00107

Made in the USA
Lexington, KY
30 June 2018

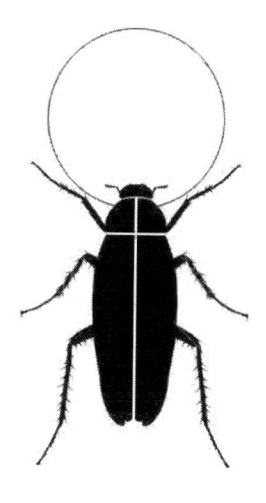

DARWIN'S BOOK OF SAINTS

ALEXANDER JOHNS

Published and Distributed by Aurore Press

ISBN-13: 978-0-692-11604-3

FIRST EDITION

aurorepress.com

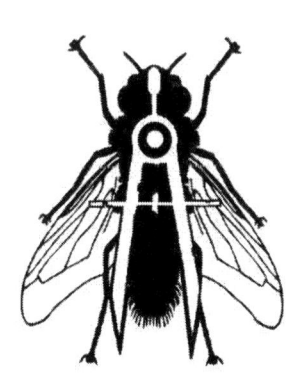

EXOSKELETALISM

Variation Under Domestication

"We can allow satellites, planets, suns, universe, nay whole systems of universes, to be governed by laws, but the smallest insect, we wish to be created at once by special act."

- Charles Darwin

SLUGGISH

I awoke before dawn
like farmers or warriors do,
elementary school teachers too,

coffeed up with NPR news
and her soothingly intelligent,
preconsidered delivery
of the day's reasons to be afraid,

got dressed and brushed and broke open
the house at the front

to go out
and get mine for my own.

Human's gotta do what a human's gotta do.

I paused in the garage, though,

looked at my feet below, just at the base
of the left front tire, to find

that slug,

going as slow
as Atlanta traffic crawls
or
the sun sets or
the moon rises or
a child grows or
an ideology takes hold of a nation

(Sorry to take so long with that simile).

At any rate, despite his lack of teeth or eyes,
he was clearly on the attack, driven with rage.

Inaudibly, he hissed,

Curses be upon you, human!
Death to the bringers of salt!
May your blood pressure be ironically high
for that time as a child you tortured my kind!

Die, motherfucker! Die!

LOST

I was so focused on the writing that
I noticed not
that a roach had lighted,
ninja-quiet,

on my bald skull,
my light bulb with ears:

an armored astronaut now perched
upon a virgin surface.

At least a minute had passed,
(perhaps a day in a bug's life)

before I felt it make its way
from my crown down my spine. I

raged and flailed as effectively as
a ninja on Xanax, and
when it fell, despite its skill, revealed
there on the arm of the chair for what it was,

alien, exoskeletal,
almost black,

I slammed down my fist
and in the process hit the black X
in the corner of the screen
to end the software's session,

and I lost the poem,

the best one I've ever written.

This story is literally true.

The poem would have been truer,

the way stars each scream
a secret,

the way every dream
seems to be an example of something,
but you can't know what just yet,

perhaps primordial chaos,
perhaps of future times,
perhaps of something
psychic, extinct, or otherwise
divine.

Then you forget.

A WELCOME BREAK FROM ETERNITY

The monastery dared gravity, leaning off the cliff.
The building itself was an act
of faith, tree-limb triangles
supporting floors and walls
floor pallets, pots and pans,
manuscripts, relics, and
some men, accessible only
by a miserable, many-mile
trek up a never-ending incline
in the never-blind blazing sun;
or god forbid the ropes
hanging like woven tears
down the crags to the rocky
coast and ocean a mile below.
Having opted for the former, I
stood, sweating and breathless
in the entryway for what
seemed like forever
before a figure finally
descended the stairs,
seemed to float
with ghost grace,
a black robe broken
only by gauzy wisps
of beard. He smiled
for too long, then observed,
You are American. I lived in America many, many
years in the past. Tell me, how did things work out for that Richard Nixon guy?

QUESTION

If an octopus scuttles and glides
across the ocean floor where
the light can't reach

in a child's football helmet,

does it make an occurrence?

The currents go unnoticed much more
than most of the time. Still,
they define the patterns of life

on every land, their tentacly hand
conducting bands of air and
temperatures everywhere.

Everywhere a tree falls
there's someone there,
sometimes thousands at a time.
The question is stupid.

If a stupid question is asked
and there's no one there to hear it,
does another tree fall
in the woods?

PUBLIC RESTROOM

Just once, I want to walk into one
and find a man napping there,
another, feet up in a recliner chair
with a cup of tea,

reading *Moby Dick*,

not giving all he's got
not to look the other in the eye
to admit he's real somehow, that plank
between their penises as if
to deny another penis exists this close
to you and yours
in this shiny cold cabin

with stalls
to hide entirely
the lower forms of life
who have to shit in public.

Those horses
do it proudly

on the warm slope of a field,
the sun submitting
colors to the sky,
in brilliant combinations
even marketers can't apply
to package,

so we'll never have to buy,

behind
ancient, elegant silhouettes, steeds
dropping their clumps into that slow, happy hilltop,
raising their historic heads
through halos of katydids,
ten thousand sunsets theirs to observe.

How long have I been at this urinal?

8

THE END OF PATIENCE

The crock pot is staring straight ahead
with a fat, shell-shocked face:

logo eyes, nose of knob set on low,
brain of lean beef,
cooking slow.

Electric poet of
metal and clay skull.

Me, I'm made of
what you're thinking is meat,

my brain the fatty part, made
perhaps more interesting
by the fact

that I'm interpreting
cooking like this,

and that I once considered for hours
which part of myself I would eat first
if I were starving to death.

I settled on my large, lean calves.

Slow cooked,

they could supply
loads of protein.

MAN ON AMBIEN ON STAGE

and he's carrying a paper bag toward the microphone,
where he raises an empty-handed toast to some colleagues.

In his dream he'd come from an old-world weapons market,
purchased some artifacts he needed to explain at an academic conference,

but this was a comedy open mic,
and he'd just been to Trader Joe's,
and the first thing he pulled out
was a vacuum-packed, frozen filet of cod,
which he spun on his fingertip with surprising skill.

This killed a thousand Mongols an hour!
he declared, then stared a few of the chucklers in the eye,

grabbed a bag of all natural-snack chips,
ripped it open and flung them into the crowd.
Stars of the Desert Ninja!
he announced.

They laughed in an unprecedented way;
he was a big hit,

this man with a wife and child,
who pays his bills, does his job,
some errands when he can find the time,
sometimes prays,
and God knows he needs
more sleep than he can get.

FIVE YOGURT-COVERED RAISINS

are somewhere

in this entire pound
of Nature's Way
trail mix.

Get off the road.
and back on the trail;
be a better person; journey away

from your day-to-day,
peanut to peanut to fraction of a cashew to
sliver of coconut to
Hey, lookee here,
we've got us a yogurt-covered raisin!:

precious, sweet little egg in the less-than-delicious nest.

Bless you, brother, fellow earth dweller, for not over-stressing
the udders of a cow

or extracting more than our species' share of sugar or
oil of the palm (the harvesting of which destroys animal habitats)
to put more than a third of a handful of these treasures in here.

Must love Mother Earth,
Flower Child

with some capital
who knows here it's at,

man.

Your conscientious corporation cares
for the individual animal or plant,

leads us beyond the orchard
back into the woods

while you, the prime primate, gaze

from the mountain top
at the vista of the bottom line.

John 5:1-4 recalls the Pool of Bethesda, where when the hand of an angel troubled the waters, the first to enter would be healed of his infirmity.

VIAGRA FALLS

was the final
phenomenon
brought on
by this inconceivable
Apocalypse.

Pills tossed in the toilet
or pissed out
boil now in the rumbling thunder
and hissing mist
of ancientness,
of river
over cancerous rocks.

The antidepressants were tasteless
passing right through your filter
or into your skin in the bath
along with disinfecting chlorine and
benzene,
pseudoestrogens,
and who knows what else soaked in?

All that flows
down the drain's
dark, dirty throat.

Those ugly sea creatures
were almost gone,
Leviathan
unviolently vanquished,

the sanctuaries of old, hot concentrations of
minerals renowned as divine
long ignored.

Roosevelt never found
healing at Warm Springs.

But, yeah, the old people by the lakes
were injuring themselves
trying new sex positions.
Men in Michigan died from Priapism
(an erection lasting longer than four hours).

Certainly not worse
than dying by famine and thirst
like those in Africa would,
their rivers dried into scabbed reminders:
highways of calcified cattle remains.

At least you weren't completely depressed
about those skeletal child soldiers
guarding their poisonous, muddy puddles,

and that's its own kind of miracle, I suppose.

800-YEAR-OLD THUMBPRINT

My mom owns one. Well,
inasmuch as one can be owned.

She stole it, actually, while wandering through Beijing.

She's stolen lots of things:
a stone from Hadrian's Wall,
a brick of the Great Pyramid,
an entire, goddamned gargoyle.

She's quite the crook, a cryptocleptomaniac, let's say.

Some unfortunate man slaved
on an emperor's temple, pressed his thumb
into a clay mold for the four hundredth time that day,
pulled out a dragon-faced, terracotta disk, sent it the to the kiln,

his baby-laden wife bringing water and carbohydrates

in the form of crudely-formed noodles,
like Play Dough snakes, we presume,
based on excavations and
Marco Polo's accounts.

Eventually, it would be set in mortar
aside the others on the glorious roof
the communist workers would dismantle
posthaste before the Olympics,
glad to hand it over to a tourist for a few American bucks. What's more

interesting, though, is that she carried it all the way through
Cambodia,
past Angkor Wat

and a million fresh ghosts,

another three plane rides,
smiling her Southern lady way through customs
at Hartsfield-Jackson International,
back home.

Fresh ghosts.

LISTENING TO THE BAND NEUROSIS WHILE PAINTING THE HALLWAY GREY

It makes sense to wear headphones
while you improve your home.

What one might wonder, though,
is "How does something
called Neurosis sound?"

Right now, it's how
Humanity
enters the End;

The radiant breaks down into life! they cry
like a canyon falling in,
the gradient of paint getting thin.

They sound like
the sun
one day
changed its mind and decided
to suddenly
tumble from the sky,

the medicine men raging from every perspective,
the heaviest band there is.

Instead of a roller, I'm using a brush,
not because I'm a craftsman
or old fashioned,
clearly not,
but since I'm desperate
and determined to stay that way,
still wearing punk-rock shirts
at this age.

I remove the smoke detector
like a troubling mole,

my brush darkening the off white,
wiping out what was,

what can never be again:

You and me as we were
and
aware of where we
should have been.

That's what they sound like:
The fear the Lord arose
to sneak away in the night,

left nothing but a scribbled note,
a last honey-do list.

That's Neurosis:

music that chews you up into
your own

personal
apocalypse.

There.

Done.

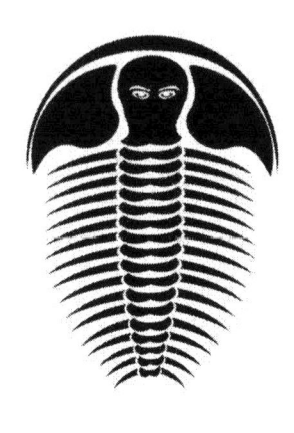

RECOGNISM

Variation Under Nature

"We must, however, acknowledge, as it seems to me, that man with all his noble qualities... still bears in his bodily frame the indelible stamp of his lowly origin."

- Charles Darwin

RECOGNISM

I crossed myself while I was
taking a piss.

I did this because
the roach was struggling for its life

in the toilet bowl.

Poor thing had no fingertips
to grip
the wet polished porcelain.

The creature was there because of me,
who'd snatched it up in tissue
and tossed it to the polluting sea.

I crossed myself because all life is holy
if not by virtue of what it is then
for what it ceases to be:

Interior exoskeleton.

I would have done the heroic insect
the dignity of flushing him or her
alone in fresher fonts,

offered a silent moment,

but I had to go really bad and
was still slightly mad at the fight
we'd just had and your frantic but
remarkably precise scramble
into to the
unreachable corners,

my flimsy cotton slipper
a disadvantaged weapon
in the fight of your life.

You don't have ears to hear,

but I cursed you during
the chase.

The Jains walk always behind
a sweeping broom, so as never
to inadvertently do you in.

They must have sensed how long
you've been around, so architecturally made
yet effective at staying alive,
no dinosaur foot nor asteroid
yet big enough
to stop your kind.

Not enough of my ancestors were so
compassionate and kind, so

here am I, Lord,
bringing the golden storm on
Darwin's greatest saint
who ain't my friend and can't be
right here and now in the bathroom at night.

I despise what I admire about you.

GETTING CORPORATE

The fleet of C-130s,
a slow drone of winged whales,
one hundred of them,

the black flock
blocking the sun
in their swell,

a city-sized shadow mass,
an unprecedented crescendo
rising
like a new virus, acquiring
the eyes of all in its path,

an actual storm of airplanes
on its way

where?

Why, to Disney World, of course,
and once they're there,

over the Holy City
of Sales itself,

they open those bay doors

at their back
and drop it,

the Shit,

metric ton after
metric ton of

every species of feces,

from every creature
there is:

22

pellety rat craps
to elephant piles,
white turds of birds to
man-sized monkey dumps,
a virtual Noah's Ark of excrement
doing more than splattering, indeed
shattering, flattening,
topographically redefining the whole damn place.

Have a dark, foul rain in your face, Disney!
Straight in your cartoon-perfect-
planet-shaped face!

CASH VALUE

I accidentally dropped a nickel in the trash,
paused, thought, then opted not

to put in my hand. You might have done the same. Hell,
it's five cents slightly defined by President Lincoln's profile.

My dad with his bald head and prominent nose
watching the evening news and
silhouetted in the window
was identical to that of
George Washington on our quarter,

the amount an elderly neighbor paid
a ten-year-old me
for mowing his yard.

History's face made monetary,
denominations of five forever associated with
the Great Emancipator's
voiceless words over a print of Gettysburg.

By this point, an attentive spender will have remembered
that Lincoln is in fact on the empty penny. That thick nickel
belongs to Jefferson, the slave owner, lecher,
wealthy expert in political theory,
etched in the pantheon
of rich dead white men.

My fellow Americans,

I was living in the Balkans
during what some called a civil war.
What it was was genocide

for nothing more than
creeds and bloodlines,

Beelzebub's ugly mug out in the open.
Saw a priest pour holy water
on prepped artillery shells.

A boy on the street handed me a handful of bank notes,
thick as a deck of cards,
hissed in perfect English,
Here, Yankee, wipe your ass with these.

EASY TARGET

That state trooper who
guides the dog and lets its angry teeth loose
on the child in her white church dress

by the firemen with the hose
firing
a skinny boy into a wall,

sits dribbling now in his dinner
on Medicaid in the nursing home.

By now, he's seen himself over and over again
on TV. Classrooms the world around

capitalize on his moment to show
just how low we can go, how far we've come.
He is

history's enemy. That day, though,
he was somebody's hero.

Filial love isn't his friend,
but who gives a shit about him?

His time in the sun,
the black and white
shadow and light.

So much color now,
so many dimensions.

He wonders about the young,
the games his grandchildren
play on the luminous screens with
graphics more real than seen,

earning points for destroying caricatures
wiping out stereotypes who reappear.

Sleepful now he dreams,
hears the screams and searches the corner
for his score
counting up.

THE PRICE OF ATTENTION

You could hear.
You could listen.
Or you could breathe in the sound alone,

let it settle into the center of you,

quiet into your heart
and re-emerge across your flesh in fresh waves,

your new knowledge of crickets and how they
communicate. The slightly flat tire

on the semi two miles away
arriving across the night to your right
ear's right ear, becoming
clearly what it is, what it
indicates.

To attend to the details
means they mean more
than anything
else:

the fly who follows me from
one room to the next, to the next,
to the next
has something to say,

so today I shut my mouth.

THE SCIENTIST

Your left eye
is a moon.

Your right a lighted
cloud.

Your nose the mast of a ship.
Your mouth

the horizon line, and I
see more,

like a cartoon version
of the creation of the universe.

I know what you are
while you stay

in two dimensions.

I don't know all the facts,
but I know lies when I see them.

There might be more bald
believers than fat atheists.

The problem consists in
how to design an experiment, since
you can't empirically define
either one.

I'm on a lone beach,
staring at a dark sea,
and I can
smell
your
beliefs.

THE BRAIN IS NOT THE MIND

Any fool with an aquarium and
half a brain can see
that any study on the duration
of fish memory

is bullshit.

Ten seconds, my ass.

They rush to the glass whenever they see my face;
they recognize their god and know
the source of their food,

and they love when my eyes
form from silently present,
unaccessed hope

to grey blur to
ghostly shape to
clearly the remembered one

who sent the manna last time

snowing down in elegant slow motion
just enough to satiate
but never pollute the tank.

Thanks displayed solely in the golden dance
of dining with the joy of multiplied loaves.
When they pass before the light,

I can see right through
to the soft dark shadow
of their hearts.

COOKING SAUSAGE ON SLEEPING PILLS

And the greatest sun I've ever conceived of
breaks above the cliffs I'm climbing,
apparently,

a Dreamsicle sun,
vanilla and orange,
and the bright electric eye of the stove
cooks the corner of my hand
(a scar I won't understand),
and the plate cracks from the heat.

It's best to use stainless steel, not ceramic,
to cook pig meat.

Pork clouds form from
the white volcano mouth
like thoughts to be consumed,
but never in full, hogs

tumble like confetti from the edge
into the Sea
of Galilee, me

eventually asleep
in a sinking boat.

EXISTENTIONISM

Struggle for Existence

"It is not the strongest of the species that survives, nor the most intelligent that survives. It is the one that is the most adaptable to change."

- Charles Darwin

CAMBRIAN SEA

For 250 million years
the trilobites ruled;
not a bad run

for some
armor-plated arthropods here much longer than and
long before the Godzillas
rose, strode, and were mown down
in a firestorm and subsequent multimillenial winter

before

our first annual think-like-a-centipede day became think-like-a-centipede-
week,
hundreds of thousands of decades
before the epiphany
that we move faster on fewer feet.

(Our focusing eyes and prey said so).
Scale softened toward feather.

Before the oceans finally overflowed their potential,
and the Galileo

of the fish dipped his
eyes into the air,
the longer-flippered Abraham
tasted the fact

that what was certain death

could be heaven,

shedding an exoskeleton once and for all,
the light took form and seemed to swim across the sky.

The moon must be an egg
in the almost infinite
silence
of an until-then

unbreathed air,
the Spirit hovering

above the water,
inhaled into fresh flesh.

The faith it takes
to stay on that shore or

step away from that boat,
reaching for that
impossible hand,

woundable and
standing on the waves.

In the moment's drop,
the armor-plated anthropod

conquered the universe
of an armorless god.

FLY PROBLEM

I can't distinguish the fly
who's lighted on the bright TV
from the fly in the documentary
about Afghanistan landing on
the back of the elderly man
handcuffed with a bag over his head.

There's the helicopter far off in the sky,
the precise size of the other flies, one alive
in my house, and one long gone by now, having
expired, had its insides eaten out by other flies,
and its hull crushed to dust
near Kandahar.

I know what a fly tastes like;
the one in my Quick Trip coffee
spent enough time in my mouth
for its flavor to reveal what it was
before I thought to spit it out:

soil and ash and something
almost metallic
with compound eyes.

NYQUIL ON PANCAKES

And it wasn't the worst thing to happen that day,
if you could call that a day.

If there's one thing that's clear,
it's that not every day is a day;
some days are seasons,
like a fortnight trudging through sand.
Some are almost okay. Once in a while you're surprised you feel alright.

Some days you're caught in the emotionscape of the night's dream.
You know what I mean,
the one in which you've lost your child in a crowd
or found his hat by a hole in the ice,

a feeling a whole day can't shake.

Some are spent staring idly into the screen's
second-hand light
sort of doing things,
though with no material result.

Other daylike things tempt you to believe
in a capricious god:
the litany of bad luck, the perfectly terrible timing
of the 120-year-old hillbilly whipping his
thirty-year-old pickup in front of you,
no one else on the goddamned road, so he can go
twenty under the speed limit, while you're
in a hurry to get to work, because you overslept
because you couldn't shut your mind down at two,
because who cares what a day means?

The patron saint of the sleep deprived
having finally nodded off.

It didn't taste bad enough to signal its
inappropriateness, the Nyquil, that is,
and it was sitting right next to the maple syrup
on the table, along with a shitload of unopened mail,
the crusty plate from yesterday,

the unopened pack of
roach traps.

The carbo blast from the pancakes
gave way to the slow-motion swim through
the senses, the tripling of your body weight

that would be that kind of a day,
one in which you sleep three hundred
and sixty five times
but only for three seconds each.

WATCHED BY RATS

That's right; they
waited for me at night
behind the dumpster. They knew

the good bag would come,
like a swollen udder
I'd drag from the apartment
to heave over the rusted rim
from the furthest possible distance
before I ran

from their red eyes
and bald tails. They
attacked babies as far as I could tell
from GBH (Look 'em up)
and from the film adaptation of Richard Wright's
Native Son.

I once shouted curses at one
waddling along the subway rail
in the rush hour station.
The commuters all assumed
I was a lunatic.

"Look at that goddamned thing!" I screamed
and cringed, but they were all looking at me.

Fools.

AMERICAN REALISM

Jack London was well hung.

Though he wasn't a large man,
he was well endowed indeed. He was
a good writer, not the greatest,
but a more-than-capable American
realist. I'm not speaking figuratively here;

his penis was disproportionately huge.

No one has yet mentioned this interesting bit
of trivia, and it's essentially irrelevant,
and of no literary value.

I'm aware of this odd fact
because I happened to see a photograph of Jack in the Klondike,
and it was impossible not to notice the motherload
in his overalls.

And it's nice to be recognized
for something other than your art.

ENTREPRECISION

Not-quite men
with sharpened sticks

moved in on
an American Mastodon.

Thirteen feet from foot to crown
with javelin hooks of stone on its face,

stuck then chased the furious beast,
which struck then crushed more than one

of them. Five not-quite-five-foot primitives

finally bled the warm life from the ruler of cold land,

then chanted and danced

and dismantled two tons of
fur, muscle, and bone of vanquished god

with hand-held, sharpened stones.

Clovis men
buried the heart the size of a beachball in dirt,
set the penis in the fire.

All ate by flame 'til they were in a coma.

When they woke, they told miraculous tales
of language, trust, hunger, and love,
the elements essential,

the earth, air, water, and fire of survival.
The whetherness of the weather,
desires of the beast man in the sky
for once seemed to align with theirs.

Weeks of celebration ensued.
After all,

father of father had been brave enough
to take on the monster on and failed,
but son of son finally saw
that the life source was between the arms;
he volunteered to run under and lift the shaft.

He would become their priest
and their breeder.

His ego would lead him
to voice opinions about the sun.

I never use my canine teeth
in a canine way, though they help me
keep my nails short,
nor my feet to chase prey,
though they get me to the car,

and I'll drive with thoughts on my mind,
failures replayed,
biological desires,
scenarios' worst-case.

Explorations of nomad mind.
Not since the ages of cave sleep
has silence filled languageless air.

Not since sex and constellations were the best entertainment
have we been truly together.

Without the other,
one simply can't launch
into to the outer space
of the inner self.

KILLING ANTS WITH ERIK SATIE

Who can save them from me?
Their eyes not right to see a man

and ears without to hear the strains
of Erik Satie,

who provides the score:
Gymnopedies
numbers 1, 2, and 3.

Me, I'm the movie
itself as I

carry to the sink
that sticky spoon that drew them in
wash a few to
watery deaths
then

place the sweet, toxic drops
in its spot
on the counter, some more
by the door where they're entering.

They pass it by for a while before one
stops to sip.
another comes, seems to
watch then move in,
a pair at the pool.

Soon they're surrounding it,
little black pencil tips
radiating out
like a child's drawing of the sun.

Coming down the white baseboard
they are fallen chords
a long song, a largo
stepping along
the path,
the staff
to the ritardando,

a slow, open melody
to the nest
to offer the queen
the rest,
the grave.

AIR HOCKEY IN THE LESBIAN BAR

Atlanta, 1996,
the year of the Olympics.

Don't ask me how Scotty found it,

the air hockey table, that is.
Just called and said,
"Let's go drink and play air hockey."

Scotty didn't come across as bright,

but he was very beautiful,
not that I could tell, other than by how
the girls fainted in his wake.

They weren't particularly happy about it,
the ladies at the bar, but we played hard.
Our dollars bought beers.
We cursed and cheered.

And the sisters who'd scowled at first when we entered
began to watch:

Got you there, pretty boy!
Don't lose to the dork!

Pretty sure that was me.
The competition intensified:

The winner gets a beer on me!
Some cash changed hands:

My money's on the smart-looking one.

Bad bet.

Both Scotty and I
had thrown the ashes of our best friend
into the air at a cliff's edge, and
the sticky bone stuff stayed in our palms,

which we slapped together like Pontius Pilate
before the crowd, and when I cried a few minutes
later, Scotty snatched the tissue from my hands and threw it
into the abyss then chuckled and grinned.

I've never felt such comfort since; he was an expert at whatever that was,
his older sister having been murdered by a jealous lover,
his father a violent drinker,
his mother a bucket of worms
writhing in a charismatic church.

Scotty just needed to beat someone at something,
and he beat me at grieving and air hockey,
and it brought him some peace,

and let me be the first to thank the lesbians for that.

CHRIST GRILLING FISH

which he did, didn't He?
Over burning wood there on the shore

after air returned to his lungs
and His disciples
floated in their boats
and tumultuous thoughts.

John Chapter 21 somewhere.

Had he caught them
using a line and a pole?
Extended to miracle
them into existence then
cut out their guts
and lay them
over the coals,

silver bodies turning black?

He fed his friends,
hungry from an unproductive trip,

perplexed,

tearing bread to eat
what they couldn't catch.

THE SMELL OF PROGRESS

Rhinoceros Ass
perhaps
five feet away

looks like a dry cow pie, the
underside of a crab
and a grey Rubric's cube
got it on in a Marvin Gaye way
and gave birth to

a body part.

Hind quarters with layers.

I can smell it too,
the rich stench
an olfactory connection
to prehistoric beasts
my distant ancestor
fled from or killed
for food, who saw this view
and was filled with hope or joy:

animal caged or running away,

the smell of progress.

This one lacks the human decency to turn around
and reveal his true length,

much less offer us a glimpse
of the weapon between his

confusing eyes

in the L.A. Zoo.

LIFE OF SLICE

The smallest sliver on the pie chart,
an eyelash on an eyeball,

the visible participant in being gladly removed,
the taxpayers' commitment to their
public school teachers there
but slowly disregarded, as stupidity
doesn't feel so bad down the throat.

Mascara sales in the San Fernando valley
have tipped the scales since the '90s
when it became the epicenter
of porn.

Across the board it doesn't amount to much,
like it does one week at the high-priced-escort service
during the annual corporate retreat in Vegas.

See the powerpoint. See the stick
attached to the suited arm
attached to the chlorinated smile
and hairful head.

What he said, what he said
when he shook your hand or
swung that wood
in a perfect circle

and drove the tiny, white, moonlike ball
so far downrange, it flew
like a comet,
while you
got lost in the
gorgeous composition

of cumulus clouds against
the trees with that
slight breeze.

Then came to yourself
and agreed to a date for lunch.

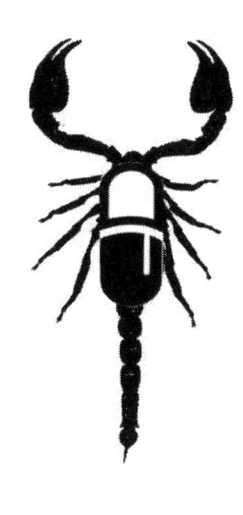

EXTINCTIONISM

"Man tends to increase at a greater rate than his means of subsistence."

- Charles Darwin

THE GROUPIES DON'T SHOW UP FOR THE FIRST TIME IN FORTY YEARS

and Gene Simmons stands, staring at the back stage door,
a feeling

he's never had before, the arthritis in his hands
can't hold a candle to the sperm
churning in his balls with no clear destination

after his bass playin' and blowing fire (his other job).

Samuel Barber's "Adagio for Strings" starts up
somewhere, but it's not that scene from *Platoon*

that plays, not Willem Defoe dying in slow motion, no,

its Gene's penis going lifeless,
despite the fact that
Viagra sponsored the tour.

A tear forms at the red edge
of his eye
then tumbles through the
black paint, Tammi Faye-like

into the white,
and he turns,
bat wings aslump,
stepping slow
in his snake-faced boots

to the bathroom stall.

TOSTITOS CHEESE DIP

tastes like LSD to me.

Not literally, of course.
Well, define "literally."

I mean, I must have had some
while tripping years ago.
It's hard to say.

But "all natural" or not,
it tastes synthetic today.

For all I know,
I was taking up a crispy disk
of the genetically-enhanced bounty of the earth
in machine-compressed form to haul from
a dense orange sea,

the green and red flecks of phosphate-preserved peppers
becoming to me
the clipper ships of Christmas,

being with my tongue
in the creamy brine,

consuming the truth
about Santa Claus
or mermaids,

the secret meaning of traffic lights,

the definition of artificial night

reaching into the jar,
its ingredient list the script
of a godless earth

upon the transparent sarcophagus
of nutrition
and of

everything else that keeps us alive.

The opposite of Communion,
Judas' hand in the dish.

What was I talking about?
Oh yes, the cheese dip.
Don't eat it.

THE BLAST THAT MAKES IT GREY

Knocking back the bottle
of vodka burning hot, my eyes

can't help but gaze
heavenward.

Here's to us

and the new grey strands
in my beard pointing up,

frozen feathers of flame,
a hundred dysfunctional flashlights,

the flares colored strange rising
from the mountain

of burning diapers,
a hundred sizes of bottleneck
or doorknob.

Something of dad must have been
added to the air if not when he died

then when I consented to have his flesh
incinerated for lack of funds.

Try for the surface of the sun,
mortician, please, my request.

Where
is the air?

In my lungs?

Blood?
Heart?
Home?

LaGuardia Airport,

where I watched a swallow
soar right past security
into the concourse,
while reclaiming my shoes
after the pat down
the day before the news?

Some quick-stop restroom in western Carolina?
Moving a dune ten miles from Timbuktu?

and your enemy's
child's nursery room? Indeed

she
ends only at the edge
of the atmosphere,

evaporation's final destination.

Where else is the air?

Must the freezing man

have lost all feeling in
his feet, face, and hands

before he's guided
to some firewood?

Place my face in the fire again,
and again I am a boy scout.

I was young.

You yearned
to make me older,

and now I'm rocking
in your old wooden chair,
and there's a bottle in my hand.

DRAWING MAZES ON ADDERRAL

And all I can imagine is
making more maze; page
snakes into page,
amphetemeaning.
the neural network of
ADD:
point

A

to

                                    point

B.

Welcome to being

                                            me.

SLEEP WIRING

Lightning strikes half a mile away,
and the microwave starts up, uninstructed,
cooking nothing but crumbs and the crust
of tomato sauce
stuck to its ceiling, its
cluttered, flat cavity of skull.

Clearly,
I've been sleepwiring again.

(That Ambien's a hell of a drug.)

I had a hunch when the thermostat
wouldn't go below 80
and the white noise machine
kept keeping time.

My concerns were confirmed by
the scribbled note in the breaker box, which read,
I am dry rot. I am wire.
in my hand

(Sleep writing again.)

I cursed and shook my head,
ran upstairs and yanked open
the medicine cabinet

and there,
staring with pure, pure meaning

was that bag
of tongue-tangy
dill-pickle-flavored
potato chips,

sewn shut.

ENGLISH

The half Chinese, half Native American man
with white dreadlocks, each one speckled
with green diamonds (not like the ones in Lucky Charms)
dripping out from his black, half burqa half priest's robe
spoke in almost English by the pool at the Turkish resort
during the complete lunar eclipse, when the clouds
resembled lumps of waning charcoal against
a black sky, and I

apologized for my native language and how bad it is
at articulating the ineffability or sublimity,
all alphabetic and shit,
nothing mystical about it.

No wonder that preacher's thumping the book.

The poet dies a drunk, no
ideogram he can find for love nor the state
of waking from a dream
in which he's visited by his deceased dad
who, upon being asked what he's been up to,
hurries away, adding
Unprocessing!

His breath a muzzle flair,
his head a lack of hair.
Or love, his voice
a toy rushed into the brine.
There's no good word for what that feels like.

Reader, I'm nearing the end of the book, so
what do good words look like
on the page?

BELUGA WHALE ENTERS AFTERLIFE

The light
in the aquarium
never quite was like
that from her arctic
childhood,
frolicking ghost
in dark ocean
beneath Santa's
illusive home.

Humans, each the size
of a newborn calf
with such similar eyes

so much alike
she'd been confused as a child
and swam right up
one long summer
to the black clad ones,
and that's the last
she remembered before she woke
in the room with one window

and dark walls,
the other whale
there with her,
sharing fading memories
through chirps and clicks
of the
before life:

month-long nights
lit only by
bioluminescent fish.

More faces come
at Christmas.

(She wouldn't have put it this way,
but we have no way to say what

it meant to her).

The instinct to forgive

the few who felt the Compassion,
the Understanding stood confused,
lifted their hands to the plexiglass,
felt and spoke their shame
she drank in as evidence
of the life beyond.

Like leaves of light.

Observations of

the most Buddha like of mammals,
almost a blubber ghost

starting to bloat,
to float.

Waking
walking along a wall
of moonlight, not a
moonlit wall, mind you.

Heaven is wet feet
with a dry house in sight.

A ghost is a full moon
behind a third night of
thick cloud cover,

mist clouding lenses.

The iceberg that sank the Titanic
was
at the last minute

lit up
like a Christmas tree.

HYBRIDISM

"What is a charitable heart? It is a heart that is burning with charity for the whole of creation, for men, for the birds, for the beasts, for the demons - for all creatures. He who has such a heart cannot see or call to mind a creature without his eyes becoming filled with tears by reason of the immense compassion that seizes his heart, a heart that is softened and can no longer bear to see or learn from others of any suffering, even the smallest pain, being inflicted upon a creature. This is why such a man never ceases to pray also for the animals, for the enemies of Truth, and for those who do him evil, that they may be preserved and purified. He will pray even for the reptiles..."

- St. Isaac the Syrian

LIONESS WITH INFECTED WOUND

Reclining,

trying to stay in the shade,
continually curling her spine
to reach the pussing place
with her tongue,

unable, thirsty.

For three days she lays
where rain has ripped away
the soil under a tree,
left a roof of roots.

If Emily Dickinson were territorial,
this would be her.

HAIR OF THE DOG

A dog on opiates
will eventually get
opioid-induced constipation,
or O.I.C.
Believe me.
Do you believe me?

Ask your doctor if giving dogs drugs is right for you.
It was right for me. See,
the dog was old and in real pain.

I was kidding when I asked
my doctor (as if he's mine),

if my heart was healthy
enough for sex.

He didn't laugh,
and I remembered
that

his wife had died in a car crash.

After all,
which heart are we talking about?

Enough on that subject;
I've suffered too,
from hair loss.
My dad had the same disease,
and he's dead.

And the coroner with the hair plugs
tore his face pulling him from the bed,
offered me a platitude about a better place
and wouldn't let me see him one last time.

Ask your doctor if radical empathy
is right for you.

Hair Club for Men can
put you in a better place,
relieve your constipated ego.
Wake that dog again and swim
with bikini-clad women who'll
shine an unblemished smile
as they run their fingers through your hair.

USED CONDOM AND SHARD OF BROKEN GLASS

We drew truly cool water
from the spring.

Stones had been stacked against
the pressure of the creek

at least 900 years before, though
none of the monks could say for sure.

And what would the point have been to know?
Some men saw the future and stayed.

Cameras have never been allowed there,
so I'm using words now.

At any rate, the water was holy and cold
like life,

and the Bulgarians, who'd shared their rotgut
the night before and farted while they slept
while I could not

in a medieval building without electric light,
the night I'd spent in total black, listening to the sea
crash against the rocks

before the prayers began at three,

would shake up their ground coffee,
like whatever the white stuff is
in a snow globe, and we'd toss it back.

God bless Bulgaria;
I needed that to survive.

It would be eight before we'd eat too little and be on our way,
up the steep, steep cliffs in a lurching, rusty truck, every
passenger in mortal prayer, except for my narcoleptic friend

who'd slept in peace the night before and who slumbered now,
his slobber flinging to the window then my shirt with each extreme turn.

The man behind us leaned forward:
Your friend has died...Do you think he's in paradise?

I'm writing these lines in a Spanish Revival mansion
in the Hollywood hills,
drunk on single malt scotch,

a half-baked Hemingway

above the trashed mansion of Los Angeles.

Yesterday I ran up into the mountains
far above the city til I was very, very alone, Amen,
looked down upon the skyline

in its wedding dress of smog,

knelt and linked cornea with lens
to take it all in,
imprint it in zeros and ones.

Then, I felt that glass dig in
to my left knee, there next to the condom,
(might as well call it the Necronomicondom at this point in the poem)
wrinkled like snakeshed in the dry dirt high

above the day to day, week to week,

decade to decade, generations of
makers of illusions,

the illusion destroyed,
like the promise of family
or faith

when there's a camera around.

THE POET

- On the occasion of the first interbreeding between disparate ancient
species of hominids

Before words were, as such,
and gestures developed together with grunts
in the ritual toolkit

to communicate
among members
of the band of

neanderthals,

one manward ape awoke

in the cave where
he'd studied the sound of his own voice,
a single, repeated note
bouncing off the wall,

the god made of himself
calling back in there in
the earth's womb where

he'd eventually paint the hunt,
his hope's highest moment.

He had dreamed of
a field of butterflies
burying themselves
in the dirt. Then
the shape of her face,
that strange and wonderful shape,
that Day he

wandered off to a meadow,
collected all the yellow flowers
his hairy, opposable-thumb
hands could carry
and wove them

around a pyramid of branches:

a fire
of color and fragrance,
a cover of comfort
and safety, the

opposite of decay. He
carried her
away from the

shared kill
up the hill

to the chapel
with no name.

PISSING IN THE SAME SPOT OVER AND OVER AGAIN
LIKE A DOG WITH ALZHEIMER'S

There's more territory out there, don't you know?
You, person who might have been you.

You used to want to roam
so far so bad you'd strangle yourself

on the leash to get to nothing but the need
to get to somewhere else, poor dog
or whatever you are.

Here you are forgetting where you just were
or where you want to be,

so present in the moment of relief.

What you've got left: your
ability to slowly eat, see
the liquid through your body, pee, recognize

shape and scene
though not what they mean

or connect you to, you

close-to-blind canine Buddha being
setting down your leg,

your tail already in a coma,
your nose playing tricks on you.

You are born again again.

RELATIONSHIP WITH A SPIDER

Is a real possibility
when you find her,
in wintertime
minding three eggs in a cold basement,
alive?

She founded her web in part
on a book you need,
but to move it would mean
to wreck her reason to be:

those little spheres
suspended like tiny planets,
earth-colored fruits
on translucent limbs.

Breathe out, and she stirs.
The string-thrum music through her
feet then abdomen. A Romanian

saint spent sixteen years
in solitary confinement
with a single roach
to confide in, and he loved her who
kept him alive and sane.

They conversed,
and he gave her a name.

Were enough days permitted to pass,
The Lord would have had
to allow a taste from that Tree.

You won't disturb spider further.
She
gets to stay. The way
Love grows
in a cave.

TONE VS. PITCH

The wind is a symphony
when there are dunes or leaves

to pass through

and you listening:

tunes weaving,
the huge tapestry of the world,

its predictable cycles rendered
myth when unpredictable events occurred,

miracles, words

might capture what it meant,
might script the storm in its movement, remember

spirit and *flesh* are words as well:

weather vanes of knowing
what the wind can tell.

ROBOT CONTEMPLATES FOG

- for the artist David Noah

Does not compute would be a reasonable
metaphor for
what the robot's going through,

but the robot world is devoid of metaphor.
For that matter, robots know no world:

Which way to move?
What to do to
what's in my view?

Mother robot
manufactures her offspring.

Manufracturing is all human can
do with machine.

Scientists successfully teach gorilla
it will someday die.

Crow attacks drone.
Crow wins.

Dog sleeps under piano.
Can't believe in the existence
of Chopin.

Sound literally etched
into the cassette

next to a tinker toy
in the silverware drawer.

Robot removes tumor.
Human contemplates fog,
contemplates robot contemplating fog.

IRISES IN WIND

    - After Franz Wright

The wind will die down when I say so.

If not, my son will tear it a new one,
scream into the Pacific

with its incomprehensible gale,
waves of sand blasting skin

from his lower legs.

Everything his little lungs can beg
from his little heart he'll blare out

like bananas banding together against the monkey.

Lord willing, he'll never know
what it's like to hold a piece of newspaper up to
block the sleet storm of sleeping pills.

The wind will die down, goddammit. Die down wind!

Christ was asleep in the boat's bow
in Unoriginate dream,

and his disciples were afraid.
Oh they of little faith;

every bed is a door,
every weather system is a war.

When you express your best question

you'll win, then,
exhausted,
you'll lay your body down,

and the wind will die.

NUN FINDS PORN STAR WITH BULLET WOUND

And isn't this the fiction with the most potential
for redemption?

I had the idea when lonely and drunk
like Hemingway spent most of his life.

I know how hard it can get,
in more ways than one.
Once I awoke,
somehow,
in another state's motel;
never mind. I was glad
to be awake again.

Nun knows first aid, saves life of
Babe with double Ds.

How'd she get into this situation?
Might matter to you, but
not to
the nun.
See, she's a good one,
not the type to hit your wrist with a ruler
in school or to
try to fool you out of hell.

Purgatory is a bullet-wounded porn star.

Porn star finds nun with bullet wound,
unconscious in an alley in LA.
Knows CPR and how to apply a tourniquet,
and I'm thinking it's on the same street
where my mom watched a homeless schizophrenic
take a dump on the curb
while he argued with spirits.

And fuck it; since we're this far
into the fiction,
porn star considered the convent
but became a first responder instead,
once rode in the ambulance,
hoping to save battered women and overdose victims,
and the occasional gunshot gangster
who gets to see an angel on the way out.

I like to imagine the Insanity of Grace.
It's crazy out there on these streets.

DARWIN'S GREATEST SAINT

Do roaches hold grudges?
Carry vendettas?

Yes.

Yes they do; they flew straight at me

when I was a boy,

no one in the dark hall but us two,
no reason for the monster to move;

it chose to attack, stingerless, venomless, stupid,
to defile me simply by its touch,

risk the crush.

Those fuckers meant business, and we were at war.
I kept a can of Raid on the table by my bed
in the attic, and
many a noble roach
dropped almost dead,
epilepticexoskeletal death throes,

wriggles on the back on the wooden floor, which was almost worse
than just letting them live to make their way across my sleeping face,
reserving the nerve agent.

I'd awake with each twitch fit into its death,
each determined kick to flip and crawl one last time,
the minutes between them spacing out.

Eventually, I'd enter a dream, or a nightmare.

Even when they're finished by a shoe, the goo they express,
white guts, like puss from a hopeless human wound,
their final *Fuck you!*

Ghosts had nothing on them.
Though they followed me too,

apartment after apartment
as a young adult, along with haunted neighbors.

One who did war with demons at 2 A.M.
and never so much as acknowledged my broom handle
handled like a spear into the wall
and my *Shut the fuck up!!*s.

Motherfucker knocked one day on my door and asked me
to feed his cat while he was away.

Okay.

The first day I turned the key in the lock
and pushed on the door,

at least forty roaches fell to the floor and scatted in every direction.

It was the greatest string of expletives ever uttered,
but it was before the age of the smartphone,
so there's no proof thereof.

Inside the place, which was perfectly organized
and so tidy that there was not a wrinkle on the bed, was

- How can I describe this? -

a roach civilization;

they moved in clear currents,
like the streets of New York as seen from fifty floors up, but they
concentrated in certain regions: the kitchen sink,
the cat's bowl. It was, needless to say, foodless.

and the cat? Well,

she was hiding under the bed, and she seemed to be saying
through her slow long howl,
You moron! Get your ass under here if you want to survive!

But I'd seen days before how she'd ripped her master's face
when he reached for her under the car,
a Chevy Cavalier, the same year
as the one my high school girlfriend drove, the one
we parked away from streetlights
to make mistakes in, Evolution
having her way inside its hard shell.
In the canyon in the bridge of his nose,
flowed a river of hemoglobinly-challenged, hopelessly alcoholic blood.

I took three showers in a row,
then called the tenants together
to show them the show.

We held an impromptu meeting in the parking lot,
agreed, dare I say we bonded a bit.

And when he returned, we forced him
to commit roachicide, multiple foggers set off
like a neutron bomb, even paid for the poison ourselves.

I hoped for his health he'd slept in a motel that night,
but he didn't.

See how the roaches work?
See how they get their revenge?

THE CAT DIED ON A PIZZA BOX

flattened out on the floor.

We're lazy and sometimes miss
the recycling bin.
Bottles and cans
form more or less a pile
near the receptacle.

She didn't respond,
but retracted slightly at my touch
to reveal her final pose,
like a clumsy, fuzzy hieroglyph
in the square,
littered with grease stains and phrases
there to make you feel better
about having ordered Dominos:

The United States is home
to more than 9 million dairy cows.
What a big happy family.

Could it be the sauce?

Take your tastebuds on a tour of America.

When the van rattled away
from the refugee camp and
the ruins of spires, and a horizon of smoke
faded into the sunflower fields,

and I wiped a tear on my sleeve,

it was nothing like this.

Let's be honest;
no amount of sentimentality is going to make me
have loved nor even liked
the cat.

Cats are, regardless of the affection they show...
Cats are, despite their cozy shell...
Cats are, whenever they curl their warm selves
against your cold, bare leg...
are transparently
selfish.

But she died
on a pizza box
on an unmopped linoleum floor,
and I, and she,
had always hoped for more.

AFTER YOU

- for Aralee Strange

I followed from
the fire of friends

into the car. You knew
the way home, but
you swerved,
a suggestion of asphalt,
lines are for crossing,
fuck the police.

Let 'em join the parade,
etching your seismogram,
a mountain range or
the EKG of the city on the street.

You'd been to that brink more than once,
and I halfway hoped for the strobe
of blue glow
to hear what you'd say
as the patrolman leaned in
then further, then squatted at the window,
lowering his light, removing his hat.
what is Law?
In the face of Art?
Make each road your own Van Gogh.

Or was it the last dream I had?
The one I could put a title on.

About the day I make my decision
to erase your messages.

And the bearded one spoke no words,
the bearded ones spoke no words.
Til the time.

I decide

to make you a falling echo,
drift into the holding cell of personal history
where you'll wait for me, shadow
mother, wait.

Where I wander in the vision

into that luminous auditorium to find you
where you always belong,

unhealthy in a holy way,
shrouded in cloth not-quite white,
coughing out souls,
taking flight,
humming and bright,
relentless and pure.

I woke again there,
where you left us
conversing with coals.

Alexander Johns is an Associate Professor of English at the University of North Georgia, where he teaches creative writing and American literature. He was born and raised in Atlanta, Georgia and currently resides in the Athens, Georgia area. He is the recipient of the 2013 Pavement Saw Press Prize for his collection *Robot Cosmetics*, and his poems have appeared in *Town Creek Poetry*, *Stray Dog Almanac*, *Chaffin Journal*, *Accents Publishing*, *The Oklahoma Review*, *Red River Review*, *Two Drops of Ink*, *The Journal of Language and Literacy*, Kota Press, Scrivener's Pen, Bellemeade Books, and other publications and were featured in the No Small Measure Georgia Broadsides project. He is the managing director of Word of Mouth, a monthly reading series bringing together nationally known and local writers in Athens, Georgia.

ACKNOWLEDGEMENTS

"Relationship with a Spider" and "Tone Vs. Pitch" appeared in *Town Creek Poetry*
"The Poet" appeared in *The Journal of Language and Literacy Education*

Cover image by Alec Grefe, aka Astronaut Husband.